Praise

'Remarkable, insightful and inspirational in equal measure.'

— **Matt Parker**, CEO, Babble

'As a self-professed, perpetually stressed multi-tasker, I was immediately drawn to *The Uni-Tasking Revolution* with hopes that it would help break my propensity to juggle twelve things at once while being fully aware that I'm wasting tons of time. To my great delight, the book has shown me how to break away from my deeply embedded habits and re-focus my energy on what's most important, *when* it's most important. Sarah Furness's incredible talent for telling relatable stories (and who doesn't love good fighter-pilot stories?) makes her lessons and improvement tactics instantly memorable and an absolute blast to read!'

— **Ken Schmidt**, former Communications Director, Harley Davidson

'In this outstandingly relatable and sincere book, Sarah Furness takes the reader on a journey of understanding and action. Having been a Commando pilot, a stressed banker and a mindfulness teacher, I wish this book had been written years ago. It should be mandatory reading for many.'

— **Tim Boughton**, Founder, Elios Partnership

'Sarah Furness does it again in her second book, *The Uni-tasking Revolution*. In a funny, joyful way, she coaches us, showing how uni-tasking enables us to become brilliant. She gives guidance on how to maintain that brilliance and be the best version of yourself – whether managing your clients and people around you or completing daily tasks. If you want to be a top performer, read this book.'

— **Siobhan Brookman**, Executive Client Director, Sopra Steria

'*The Uni-tasking Revolution* made me laugh out loud. Reading Sarah's words made me realise that, actually, I can do this. I can take things one step at a time and teach my brain to focus if I follow the simple steps in this book.'

— **Jo Ritchie**, Senior Business Manager, Vodafone

'*The Uni-tasking Revolution* is brilliantly structured and packed with entertaining anecdotes, useful diagrams and truly valuable takeaways that I am confident I can implement into both my work and my personal life. As always, Sarah Furness makes me feel like I can kick down doors with her words of encouragement!'

— **Emma Lund**, Events Lead, Together

'Sarah Furness continues to challenge our preconceived ideas with great insight, evidence and humour, openly sharing her personal experiences and providing us with a step-by-step guide to building the uni-tasking habit. This book is a must-read and the nudge I needed to relinquish my multi-tasking mindset. Who would have thought a personal development book could be such fun?'

> — **Tracey Cross**, Legal and Business Adviser,
> Empower Women Chair

'Uni-tasking has been a game-changer for me. I am constantly juggling multiple tasks, struggling to focus and leaving my door open to "bubble-buts". The tone of this book is incredibly engaging and authentic, making it feel like Sarah is right there, guiding me through the chaos.'

> — **Gary Kershaw**, Country Manager,
> Qatar Airways

'We all spend our lives doing, without ever thinking about how or why we do what we do. This book gave me the space to think about how I can "do" better. Packed with practical tips and clarity of thought, *The Uni-tasking Revolution* is more than a book; it's a movement – one which I am certainly part of now!'

> — **Nick Gold**, Managing Director,
> Speakers Corner

'Easy to use and practical, *The Uni-tasking Revolution* offers superb insight into how to drive balance and focus in your pursuit of personal growth. Sarah Furness has written a book packed with useful tips, gained from her experience of teaching people the art and science of high performance.'

> — **Jamil Qureshi**, Performance Psychologist

'Sarah Furness takes readers on a captivating and transformative journey, moving from the cockpit of a helicopter to the cockpit of our own lives. The core concept is straightforward yet profound: our attention can only be focused on one thing at a time, and mastering this focus is essential for achieving exceptional performance in both our personal and professional spheres. *The Uni-tasking Revolution* serves as a practical and engaging guide, offering a powerful tool to cut through the distractions of modern life and reach your highest potential. Whether you're grappling with everyday interruptions or seeking to elevate your performance, this book is an indispensable resource that lays out the path to a more focused, productive and fulfilling life.'

— **Natalie Maddox-Hussain**, Co-founder, Women Empowering Defence

'In *The Uni-tasking Revolution*, Sarah Furness has given us an invaluable guide to tackling the complexities of work and life – one which goes to the heart of dealing with the many pressures we all take on, then complain about. By introducing us to the HABITS method for rebalancing ourselves to prioritise effectively and focus on one thing at a time, Sarah gives us all the opportunity to deliver better, more consistent outcomes for ourselves and those around us. It turns out that less stress and better performance are indeed possible!'

— **Mark Gallagher**, Formula 1 Executive

'*The Uni-tasking Revolution* resonated with me at a personal level and helped bring clarity to my thinking. As a coach and mentor to quite a large community, I know that the learning and exercises in the book will be of great value to many – whether they are reading alone or working through activities together. Highly recommended. I, for one, will lead by example and ensure I fly the aircraft.'

— **Kim Webb**, Team Leader, banking

'In *The Uni-tasking Revolution*, Sarah Furness brings her unique blend of mindfulness and military precision to offer practical, actionable advice to enhance productivity and wellbeing and challenge the multi-tasking mindset. Her real-life anecdotes make complex concepts easy to understand and apply. I highly recommend this book for anyone looking to optimise their performance and lead a more focused life.'

— **Christopher Digby**, Executive Director, insurance sector

>>> Focus on what really matters, <<<
get stuff done, waste less time

THE UNI-TASKING REVOLUTION

Kathleen
You've been AMAZING!
Thank you.
Sarah

SARAH FURNESS

R^ethink

First published in Great Britain in 2024
by Rethink Press (www.rethinkpress.com)

For Tim, for not being a bubble-but.

Contents

Introduction

Whether you're a business owner, solopreneur or high achiever, you likely want to do more with less – and do it more quickly. Maybe you want to scale up your business, but you don't yet have the time or money to employ others. Maybe you're working as hard as you can, but you're not getting the recognition you deserve. Maybe you can see the amazing potential of the people around you, but it never quite translates to the business outcomes you're hoping for. The concept behind high performance is astonishingly simple: stop multi-tasking, start uni-tasking. That's all there is to it. Now you can close this book and go on your way.

The thing is, no matter how many times I repeat this message, good, talented, dedicated people like you are *still* multi-tasking. They may think that uni-tasking isn't realistic. I'll be honest, there have been times I've doubted myself. Should I change tack? Talk about something else? Let you continue to drive yourself towards burnout, miss the most important moments in your life and perform at 60% of your potential?

No, I bloody well shouldn't.

To understand why I'm so certain about uni-tasking you probably need to understand some of my backstory, so let's start by talking about the thing that I'm most known for and the thing I'm really, really good at: crashing helicopters.

(I sometimes wonder if I'd have anything to write about if I'd been a slightly better pilot.)

It turns out that crashing my first helicopter led me to discover the 'secret' that forever changed how I worked. It's the secret to outstanding performance and to working smarter not harder. It's the secret that underpins this book.

This 'secret' was revealed to me when I was flying a helicopter down a valley in Morocco at 140 mph just 20 metres from the ground. Low flying is hard work and bloody good fun, but the next thing that happened wasn't quite so enjoyable. The captain shouted, 'Fuck!' which was followed by an almighty bang. The canopy had shattered and air began rushing in. I was now flying a convertible with the roof down.

It transpired that we had hit wires that were strung across the valley. They were impacting in three different places: the engine intakes, the top of the canopy and squarely in the middle of the nose of the aircraft. I didn't know that then, so I was imagining these wires wrapping themselves around my tail rotor or tangling themselves up in the main rotor head. I distinctly remember thinking, 'This is how I'm doing to die,' and feeling oddly pleased that it would be a relatively quick (though satisfyingly dramatic) death. If you're going to go, you might as well do it with style.

I was roused from my self-indulgent daydream by these (now famous) words: '*Fly the aircraft!*' My attention was instantly back in the cockpit – and that was the clue to the secret. Just before I heard those words, I'd been thinking about death. How helpful do you think that was while travelling at

140 mph, when my attention actually needed to be on flying the aircraft? Not very. Why? Well, here comes the 'secret'.

Our attention can only be in one place at a time.

I'll repeat that (in case your attention wandered). *Our attention can only be in one place at a time.* Which means that where we focus our attention is pretty damn important. We need to make sure it's the one thing that actually matters in that moment. Obvious when you think about it, right? This is where you might be thinking, 'How the hell can I focus my attention on one thing when I've got a million different things I need to do in a day?'

This book is my answer to that problem. I'm taking you on the journey to uni-tasking nirvana. Because I believe in it. And I believe in you. Here's how it will work (and in big handfuls):

Phase One is the Understand phase. We will understand why it's hard to uni-task and why it's worth the bother in terms of business advantages and personal advantages.

Phase Two is where we work out how to uni-task. The job of this book is to make uni-tasking ludicrously easy, which is why I've put it into the mnemonic HABITS:

- **H**ealthy – preparing your brain to prioritise effectively

- **A**ttention – training your brain to focus on *one* thing

- **B**e in one place (a bit clunky but please roll with it) – working out how the hell to decide what that one thing is

- **I**nterferences – working out how to deal with other people interrupting our flow

- **T**rain hard, fight easy – incorporating into our routine so that it becomes a habit and therefore effortless

- **S**et the conditions – working out how to make the workplace uni-tasking friendly and how not to sabotage your best-laid plans

Phase Three is where we pull everything together and prepare you to take the lead in your own life, both for your sake and for those around you.

Don't worry, you don't need to remember all of the above. You're busy, right? Which is why, at the start of every chapter, I'll give you a 'Bottom Line Up Front' (BLUF) so that you know the point of engaging with something before you dedicate your time and attention to it. There are plenty of occasions when you need to receive a fair amount of detail to really understand something. It makes perfect sense when you've heard the entire explanation and understand why it was so important to stay engaged, but rarely is this stated upfront.

The chapter BLUF helps you determine if the chapter is relevant to you, because it tells you upfront where you are going and why you need to get there. It helps you to give your full attention to what really matters. So, I can save you time while saving you time. (If you're not fist bumping right now, then I'm doing it for you!)

PHASE ONE

UNDERSTANDING WHY

Why bother uni-tasking? Well, let's start where it matters most: our wallets.

I know we all want to be good people; we want to make a meaningful contribution to the world and die knowing that we weren't totally loathsome. But the truth is this is all a lot easier if we can make some money. This book is going to help you make more money by teaching you how to lead high-performing teams, or, if you're on your own, how to become a kick-ass solopreneur.

1

Multi-tasking Is A Myth

BOTTOM LINE UP FRONT

Uncomfortable truth:
Our brains, society and nature trick us into thinking
multi-tasking is a great idea. It's a big fat lie.

Business gains:
Get back in the driving seat and accelerate your growth.

Personal gains:
Know thyself and forgive thyself.

The secret

Let's recap on the 'secret' that I revealed in the introduction: our attention can only be in one place at a time. Once I learned this secret, everything changed. It revolutionised how I work. Because if you think about it, two important facts are obvious:

1. If our attention can only be in one place, then multi-tasking is a myth.

2. If our attention can only be in one place, it's pretty bloody important where we choose to focus it.

This gave rise to the uni-tasking definition: focus on *one* thing at a time. *Choose* that one thing. We can train ourselves to focus our attention exactly where we need it to be – indeed, this is the main effort of my work with my clients – and the good news is you don't have to meditate in a field of daisies all day to do this. Now I'll be honest, it took quite a while for that life-changing secret to bed in. In fact, it wasn't until I started studying to become a mindfulness coach that the penny dropped. I'd left the RAF and set up my company, Well Be It (www.wellbeitcoach.com).

CASE STUDY: Focus on one thing

One of my very first mindfulness clients was a GB boxer. During our first mindfulness session, he said, 'I want you to teach me mindfulness so I can stay calm when I get punched in the face.' And I thought, 'How the hell am I supposed to teach him that?' He explained, 'You must know how to perform under pressure. You've been to war, you've been shot at, you've crashed helicopters.'

I realised that I *did* know how to perform under pressure, I just didn't know *why* I knew how to do this. I started to look back through events in my military career and applying what I now understood about the brain and mindfulness. And that's when it hit me. The reason these techniques were so effective was because they were working *with* the brain, not against it. Our attention can only be in one place a time, which means that how we perform under pressure is mostly down to *where* we focus it.

What I eventually realised, would you bloody believe it, was that we had been practising mindfulness techniques in the cockpit of a helicopter. I don't mean that I was levitating like a yogi while flying down a valley; I mean, I was using mindfulness to keep my focus where it needed to be under extreme pressure. You see, it's natural for our attention to wander off. In fact, it's almost guaranteed that, under pressure, our brain will wander to just about the least helpful place it can. For example, we often focus on the things we can't reasonably be expected to control (like death), which is why, when the captain said, 'Fly the aircraft,' it meant exactly that: stop thinking about death; start doing some of that magic with your hands and feet to make the aircraft do what you want it to do.

Its relevance, though, stretches far beyond crashing helicopters into wires. What 'Fly the aircraft' really means is to focus your attention in the *one* place it really needs to be right now. So, when my dear GB boxer client asked me to teach him mindfulness so he could have the competitive edge, I realised these techniques could be applied to the boxing ring too. Then I thought, 'Wait a minute, I wonder where else these techniques might help people to perform at their best?' I started looking at my business and made an exciting discovery. I was using mindfulness to help me uni-task and it turns out that uni-tasking is a really effective way of running a business efficiently. In fact, I was able to scale up and grow the business. And grow it did.

In my first year, I made a big fat loss. In my second year, I turned over £150k. In my third year, I nearly tripled that. And in my fourth year, I was turning over more than ten times what I'd earned in year one. Lots of people would say things like:

- 'Do you have an extra two hours in the day that you're not telling me about?'

- 'You are intimidatingly productive at work.'

- 'I see you became an overnight success; what's your secret?'

Or the best compliment of all: 'So, how often are you doing the really high-paying strands of work – two or three times a month?' to which I would answer, 'Seven times a week.' At which point they would spit their coffee out and say, 'How the fuck do you fit all the other stuff in? You're everywhere on LinkedIn. You're a mother. You just got back from Santorini! What's your secret?' Without meaning to sound unbearably arrogant, the answer is simple: uni-tasking.

Why multi-tasking is a myth

Uni-tasking is completely transferable to your work routine, but (and there is a but), uni-tasking is easier said than done. It can be deliciously tempting to revert back to multi-tasking, but stick with me. I promise I'll get you there.

If you've read *Fly Higher: Train your mind to feel as strong as you look*,[1] my previous book, you'll already know why I think multi-tasking is a terrible idea. Yet we live in a world where multi-tasking is expected, normalised and even celebrated. For years, we've unwittingly subscribed to the lie that successful people are good at multi-tasking.

The truth is closer to this: successful people are falling short of their enormous potential because they are multi-tasking. Which means, if we can overcome the obvious challenges that our tech-driven world presents and commit to uni-tasking, we will be one step ahead of our competition (and so will the people in our teams).

There is plenty of science to prove that we are simply not designed to multi-task, but I'm going to recap the basic facts here about multi-tasking (check out the references included in the book for more detail).

The important thing to remember is that our attention can only be in one place at a time. Think about when we are having a conversation with someone or facilitating a training session. When we are listening to someone talking, we need to give them our full attention. We cannot listen *and* think about our response at the same time. We have to switch our attention between those two tasks, which is why we inevitably miss bits in almost every conversation we have. We divert our attention away from listening to start formulating a response in our head. When we multi-task, the brain has to switch rapidly between these tasks and fulfil additional background roles of what Meyer, Evans and Rubinstein refer to in their research as 'goal shifting' (I want to do this now instead of that) and 'rule activation' (I'm turning off the rules for that and turning on the rules for this).[2] These drain our cognitive capacity. Think about when your laptop starts to whirr at you because you've got too many programmes open at once. This is what's going on in your brain when you're multi-tasking.

Evidence shows that multi-tasking reduces our output standard by 40% (or increases our error rate by 40%), accounts for around two hours of wasted time every day and increases our stress levels.[3] Not only does that mean we feel frazzled when we multi-task, but it also has an impact on our performance, because the brain, rather unhelpfully, puts itself into fight or flight mode. When that happens, it prioritises information from the survival part of our brain, so we lose the ability to think rationally, prioritise effectively, problem-solve, access long-term memory and regulate our emotions.

You can probably see now why multi-tasking has a compound negative effect on us: if the 40% reduction in performance wasn't enough of a kick in the face, losing our shit in the middle of a board meeting or prioritising *everything* as urgent important and ending up with an astronomical to-do list is only going to make things exponentially worse.

Bottom line: no one is designed to multi-task. Not even women.[4] If I were a conspiracy theorist who hated men, I might suggest that the myth women are better at multi-tasking was invented by the patriarchy to keep us from outperforming our male colleagues. But I'm not a conspiracy theorist. And I'm rather fond of men. The truth is closer to this: society has accepted the idea that women are better at multi-tasking, and because the brain looks for evidence to support beliefs (even if they're false), as women, we've become resistant to the idea of ditching multi-tasking. I get it. Nobody likes having something they are 'good at' taken away from them. The truth is that we are doing ourselves a disservice by trying to spread ourselves thinly across multiple focus points. Multi-tasking is not helping us. It's holding us back.

What, then, is the answer? Simple. Stop multi-tasking. Start uni-tasking. How do we do this?

- We focus on *one* thing at a time.

- We *choose* that one thing.

As I said previously, uni-tasking is hard, so let's work through some of the challenges. Come on, it'll be fun.

Why is it so hard to uni-task?

Heads up – there's going to be a lot of uncomfortable truth bombs ahead. Partly because I like to think of myself as courageously honest and a little bit edgy, but mostly because it's necessary. Here's the truth: simply put, we are brilliant at getting in our own way.

Remember, the purpose of pointing this out is not to depress you. It's to free you. The starting point is to understand our barriers and then take steps to reduce their impact. Understanding our own barriers can give us a lot of insight into why others might also be resisting uni-tasking, so it can help us gain an intuitive sense of what the people in our team might need from us. Equally, as solopreneurs and business owners, it can help us to understand why those around us are not able to buy into our uni-tasking time. Whichever way you look at it, uni-tasking is emotionally intelligent leadership and entrepreneurial skills at their best – that's why the Understand phase is so important.

Here's an exercise you can do to find out how you are currently getting in your own way. Don't worry, as I said, it's fun, kind of. Enlightening, definitely. And it'll save you loads of time down the line.

EXERCISE: The five whys

To extract the maximum value from this exercise, find a time when you are least likely to be disturbed, and/or minimise the distractions (start by turning your phone face down) and give yourself 20–30 minutes of full attention.

Start by writing down: *'I find it hard to uni-task because...'*

Look at the statement you've written and see where you have placed yourself in Covey's Circle of Influence (things you have some control over) or Covey's Circle of Concern (things you cannot control)?[5]

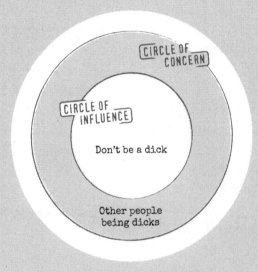

The Circles of Influence and Concern

If you write about *other* people's behaviours, you're putting yourself in a poor position to take positive action. For example, you might have written, 'I find it hard to uni-task because other people interrupt me.' You can't rely on people to magically stop interrupting you, so if that's the problem you want to solve, you need to work out what *you* can do about it.

Try and rewrite the statement using 'I' language. For example, *'I find it hard to uni-task because... I get distracted by other people.'*

Now it's time to dig deep. Developed by Japanese inventor and industrialist Sakichi Toyoda, the Five Whys exercise helps us to really drill down to the root cause of the problem.[6]

To do this, channel your inner toddler and repeatedly ask yourself 'Why?' five times. This works best if you add 'why' to the previous answer, as follows:

1. Why do you get distracted by other people?
   (Remember to write the next answer in 'I' language.)
   'Because I have an open-door policy.'

2. Why do you have an open-door policy?
   'I need to be immediately available to my team.'

3. Why do you need to be immediately available to your team?
   'Because I don't think they can do it without me.'

4. Why don't you think they can do it without you?
   'Because I haven't given them enough training.'

5. Why haven't you given them enough training?
   'Because I am secretly scared of becoming redundant.'

Go ahead, try it yourself. *I find it hard to uni-task because...*

By understanding your barriers identified by the Five Whys exercise, you gain a few advantages. You may have identified an area in your business where you need to channel your effort. For example, you might realise you need to upskill your team or give more time to training so that they don't rely on you as a single point of failure. Or perhaps you need to upskill yourself to take your solopreneurship to the next level. If understanding your barriers helps you to discover a need for training then you will ultimately benefit from being able to steer your business more strategically.

If you've been really brave and dug deep, you might have discovered a mindset barrier. These are the barriers we put in our own way. This is actually great news, because it means we can also take them out of our own way. For example, a lot of people don't like relinquishing control or are worried if they choose *one* thing to focus on that, they'll choose the wrong thing and the world will end. If this sounds like you, don't worry; you're not alone. In fact, that leads me on to the next point.

You can also use your barriers to understand what other people's barriers might be. This can help you work together to overcome some of the most common barriers. Let me share the most common barriers I encounter when I deliver workshops on uni-tasking. In the next chapter, we're going to start with one of the biggest barriers we put in our way: our mischievous wandering minds.

Key takeaways

- The biggest barriers to our success are actually the ones we put up *ourselves*, not the ones that are created by others or our environment.

- If you're able to get in your own way, you're able to get out of it, too.

Commitment to action

Complete the Five Whys exercise above so you can understand what's getting in your way. Then get excited about getting out of your own way.

2

Common Barriers And Why It's Worth Overcoming Them

BOTTOM LINE UP FRONT

Uncomfortable truth:

Our brains resist us even when it's the 'right' thing
to do. If we want to uni-task for better performance,
we need to train our brains to do things which
are counterintuitive.

Business gains:

Understanding the problem is vital in
developing a complete solution.

Personal gains:

If you've been beating yourself up for being rubbish at
uni-tasking, it's time to give yourself a break. You're
not broken. You're a bloody marvellous human being.

The challenge

Let's have a look at the five most common barriers that
tend to come up during my workshops and why it's worth
overcoming them.

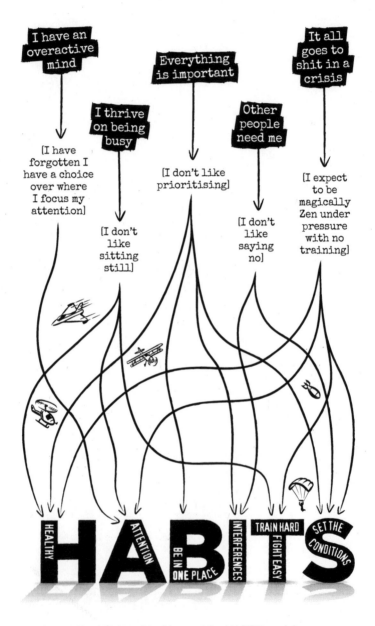

Barriers to uni-tasking and the HABITS model

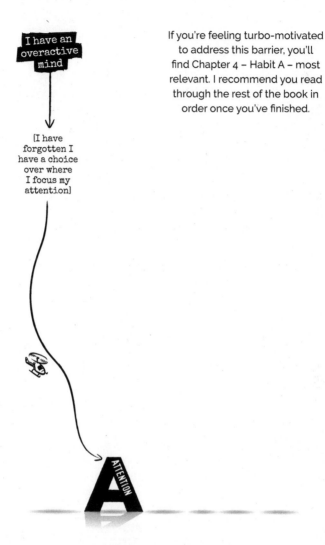

I have an overactive mind

[I have forgotten I have a choice over where I focus my attention]

If you're feeling turbo-motivated to address this barrier, you'll find Chapter 4 – Habit A – most relevant. I recommend you read through the rest of the book in order once you've finished.

Barrier 1: I have an overactive mind
(I have forgotten I have a choice over where I focus my attention)

Often, people say to me, 'I'm easily distracted,' or, 'I have a short attention span.' When we overlay the outside world, it's not hard to see why this is a major problem. You see, technology has made it possible for us to be *everywhere at once*. Which means there's now a societal expectation on us to be *everywhere at once*. (Have you noticed the creeping sense of rejection we feel when we see two blue ticks on WhatsApp and are not rewarded with an immediate response? I've turned my blue ticks off in order to save my sanity and my relationships.) Because of this expectation, we are constantly being distracted. Whether it's the multiple communication channels we have open, other people disrupting our flow, or even just our frenzied minds ruinously ruminating about the past or the future, staying focused on one thing is *hard*.

It's not surprising that we find ourselves darting from one task to the next, but this can cost us dearly. This is why most people will give up on uni-tasking and continue to underperform. They assume that there is something which renders uni-tasking impossible for them. This is simply not true, but it's a great example of the lies we tell ourselves when we are getting in our own way.

Don't worry, there's no need to feel bad about this. Remember, our brain is *always* trying to protect us, so being easily distracted or having a short attention span isn't a design flaw. It's part of our highly tuned defence system. Think about it – if we had the ability to tune out all distractions and stay focused on one thing for hours on end, it could lead to some pretty serious consequences. Here are some of them:

- We'd be oblivious to other people falling asleep or scrolling on their phones during our presentation, and we'd think it was the best presentation ever.

- We wouldn't notice if someone raised their hand to ask a question.

- We would forget to eat.

- We would forget to go to the loo.

- We could get run over by an oncoming truck (assuming you're working in the middle of the road, which I concede is unlikely).

The point is, we *need* to be distractable so we can notice emerging threats or a change in environment. In other words, we need to notice things. And to notice things, they need to be able to divert our attention. This is part of the human condition.

Why it's worth overcoming this barrier

The busy world that we live in creates an opportunity to gain an edge over our competition. When I say, 'gaining an edge', I'm not suggesting we have to 'do over' other people, but the sad truth is this: most people give up on uni-tasking because they've surrendered to a world full of distraction, and if those people are your competition, well, that's sad for them, but good for you. Because you won't be making the same mistake.

We'll be covering this in detail in Habit A, but here's something you can do in the meantime. *Make your choice.* When we get distracted, this is not the time to throw our hands in the air and say, 'I knew it; I can't uni-task.' When we get distracted, this is our chance to notice where our attention has gone, give ourselves a bloody good pat on the back for realising we've become distracted and then choose where we want our attention to be.

Maybe you need to switch your attention to the new object of focus. Or maybe you want to bring your attention back to where it was previously. The point is, you get to *choose.* Every time you choose where to focus your attention, you're uni-tasking. Every time you uni-task, you're training your brain to uni-task. Being distracted isn't a sign of failure. It's an opportunity to train.

This applies equally well to internal distraction (ie, our own thoughts). When we're focusing on a high-value work task, it's normal for our minds to wander. We might start to daydream about the future. We might start to recycle a previous conversation that didn't go the way we wanted or we start planning for something less important (also known as procrastination). In the case of hitting wires in a helicopter, I might start planning my funeral. When that happens, it's common to get stuck on that new train of thought because we simply forget that we can *choose* where to focus our attention. But remember, we can always choose to 'Fly the aircraft'. We can always choose to bring our attention back to where we need and want it to be. The next time you get ambushed by an unhelpful thought, try this:

- Acknowledge. Give yourself a pat on the back for noticing the unhelpful thought.

- Bring your attention back to the task in hand.

- Repeat this *every time* it happens.

Remember, every time you do this, you are training your mind to uni-task. There is literally no limit as to how many times you can do this. You might notice that you are pulling your attention back to your priority task several times a minute. That's OK. That's great, in fact. You're getting a good workout. As I said, we will visit this again when we look at Habit A later in this book, but for now, it's enough to know that Barrier 1 (I have an overactive mind) is not insurmountable, and there are some very simple ways we can learn to overcome and ultimately reduce the size this barrier.

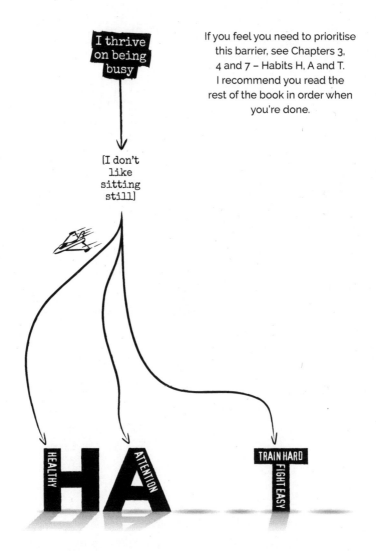

If you feel you need to prioritise this barrier, see Chapters 3, 4 and 7 – Habits H, A and T. I recommend you read the rest of the book in order when you're done.

Barrier 2: I thrive on being busy
(I don't like sitting still)

In the military, we had a phrase that repeated itself with tedious regularity: 'Hurry up and wait.' I must have spent years of my life sitting on my rucksack, waiting in a cold, damp room for the next phase of the operation or training to begin. You might assume this was due to ineffective logistics, but a lot of the time, it was deliberately imposed on us. I used to think it was because the people who planned these periods of mind-numbing boredom were cretinous masochists. But it turns out that being able to sit still conveys a huge tactical advantage. Allow me to explain.

For two years, I worked in the Joint Personnel Recovery (JPR) Cell. The purpose of my role was to coordinate a rescue mission if one of our pilots got shot down behind enemy lines (think Owen Wilson in *Behind Enemy Lines*).[7] We spent a lot of time training for this eventuality, and invariably, this training took place in a bunker deep underground. You know the rooms you see in World War Two films with a big map in the middle of the room (known, rather inexplicably, as the 'bird table') and people moving wooden planes around on it like a giant game of Risk? Well, it's a bit like that, only with computer screens. Anyway, the call would come in that one of our fighter pilots had been shot by an enemy fighter (known as red forces), had ejected and was now on the ground, possibly injured, next to a giant smoking crater where their aircraft had crashed in the middle of enemy territory. This was my big moment. I'd stand up in the middle of the operations room and shout: 'Attention on the ops floor, we've had a JPR event.'

I know that probably doesn't sound as thrilling as the Hollywood version in *Behind Enemy Lines*, but that is genuinely what I said, and everyone knew exactly what it meant: one of our guys was in deep shit. Everyone's head would turn to me expectantly, eagerly anticipating their orders on how to help me coordinate the recovery event, and at this point, I would sit back down and do nothing. Well, that's what it felt like, anyway.

You see, when we're at war with another country, we spend a lot of time trying to stay hidden from them while trying to work out where they are, because that gives us a tactical advantage. But the enemy is also pretty good at staying hidden, so rather than spending lots of time and money spying on each other, imagine if we simply set a trap, put something irresistible next to that trap, and let our enemy walk straight in.

What if the 'something irresistible' that our enemy had was one of our own pilots who needed help, alone and afraid behind enemy lines? We'd want to get them out pretty quickly, so we might send dozens of planes, helicopters and ground forces in to get that person out before the enemy got to them. Now imagine that the pilot isn't really one of our people. Imagine that the report of someone being shot down was fake, that it was actually a 'spoof' call made by the enemy to get us to send all of our forces to walk straight into an ambush. If I was the person who'd just sent all of our forces into that ambush, I'd have a lot of blood on my hands. This meant I needed to corroborate the report before taking action and there are lots of ways to do this. I won't disclose government secrets here – just know they are clever.

Even after I'd corroborated the report, however, I then had to weigh up the balance of risk, because there is no point sending multiple people to their deaths in order to try and save one. I had to know the mission had a reasonable probability of success, which meant I had to mitigate the risks as much as possible. This required further information gathering and collaboration. So, the very first thing I needed to do was to make sure I didn't send our guys on 'Operation Certain Death' to pick up a person who didn't exist.

The key point is this: this process took time, which meant I needed to be able to sit on my hands. I needed to be able to execute tactical patience and I needed to convince everyone else around me to do the same thing. This was not easy. Our brains, when we detect a threat, will *always* favour speed over anything else. Remember, even though our brains are trying to protect us, it doesn't necessarily mean that they are helping us under pressure. Our instinct will be to do something, anything, just so we can feel like we are making things happen. We will want to do something so we can feel better. As a result, we often trick ourselves into activity and mistake it for productivity. In my scenario, that is a mistake which could cost us dearly.

Why it's worth overcoming this barrier

I hope you can see now that there were some very compelling reasons why it was worth my being able to sit still in that kind of situation. If I'd rushed this process, people may have been killed unnecessarily.

In your business, rushing things might not result in people dying, but it could cost you on several fronts. Conversely, there are several reasons why your business will benefit when you hone the ability to sit still. Let's look at it from the example of selling because, let's face it, in business we are always selling, and we need people to buy what we are selling to be successful.

Tactical patience leads to better decisions

First, there will be times when you simply don't have all the necessary information to make the best decision for your customer. The temptation might be to cut corners or to come up with a best guess, and yes, that does mean you can do things quicker. It might mean you get your 'value proposition' in front of your prospect before your competitor, and I know that in the world of sales, speed of response is considered critical. But what if that means you misjudge what your customer really needs? Or if you skip through the diagnostics or don't take the time to really listen to, and understand, their problems? The product you then put in front of them could be completely inappropriate or only solve part of the problem. Not only does that mean your product is less effective than they need, but they'll also work out you weren't really paying attention to their needs and were more focused on yours (ie, to sell your product or service).

A business that's had the tactical patience to wait until they have all the information they need to present a solution that meets *all* of the customer's objectives will probably win the business and develop a better relationship with their customer, because the customer feels heard.

If sales aren't your thing, then you can simply replace 'customer' with 'your boss'. If you are a boss, don't be a dick. Let people come back to you when they have the answer.

We need to recharge

Sales is exhausting. I often draw the analogy between frontline military operations and sales because I see both as being at the 'pointy' end of what we do. It's high octane, high risk and, by definition, highly competitive. Which means we need to give ourselves time to recharge. I know that's not going to sound sexy. If you, like me, have a superhero complex and secretly believe that you run on fusion and never have to rest, then I have some sympathy. It sucks when we find out that we, too, are human, and we, too, need to recharge our batteries. But by God, we do.

There is a reason why it was legally mandated for pilots to get eight hours of sleep per night. It wasn't part of our beauty routine. It was considered a non-negotiable requirement to ensure we could fly safely and do our jobs effectively. If we flew tired, we'd make mistakes and people might die. In the same way, if you operate tired, you'll also make mistakes, and possibly lose business. And/or burn yourself out. And/or you'll spend so much time on your 'frontline' (possibly correcting mistakes that could have been avoided if you'd taken a break) that you'll forget what your family and friends look like. It's your choice, of course. But I think that's a very high price to pay for our refusal to switch off and recharge.

Sitting still brings clarity and awareness

We often don't get the answer by staring straight at the problem. Sometimes, we need to change perspective for the answer to reveal itself. That's because changing our perspective allows us to use other parts of our brain, so we can tackle a problem using *all* of our potential brain power rather than one tiny slice of it. This is why we get our eureka moments after a night's sleep, while out for a run or during a conversation about something completely unrelated. The point is good things happen when we change our perspective and sitting still can give us a whole new perspective.

Sitting still also increases our awareness. When we stop doing everything in fast-forward mode and give ourselves permission to sit still, we notice things we wouldn't previously. This might be the answer that was previously eluding us, or it might be the fact that our shoulders are completely hunched up, we are grinding our teeth or we haven't had any water for the past twelve hours. In other words, sitting still allows us to check in, not just with the solution that is waiting for us to notice it, but also with ourselves. We can thus spot when we are neglecting ourselves and getting dangerously close to burnout, which relates back to the earlier point. We need to recharge, and we need to notice when it's time to recharge before it's too late. Sitting still allows us to do both.

Sitting still prepares us for successful uni-tasking… On top of all of that (I'm in a giving mood), sitting still is training our brains for a very necessary skill we need for uni-tasking. It's training us to sit with a quiet, calm, clear mind. That might sound totally bonkers. You might think, 'Wait, I've got to *train* myself to sit with a clear calm mind?' Yes. Yes, you do.

You'd be amazed at how distrustful we can be when we feel calm. This is evidenced by phrases such as, 'The calm before the storm' and, 'If it's too good to be true, it probably is.' Most high achievers have normalised running around with their hair on fire and will distrust this sitting still nirvana level of Zen. It will feel too easy, and precisely for that reason, your brain will resist it. Expect that. And don't worry. I've got all the tips and tricks you need for your brain to accept and habitualise uni-tasking such that it becomes easy.

Try this: when things go quiet, rather than fighting it or filling it with counterproductivity, use that time far more effectively – use it to practise the skill of tactical patience. Use it to practise the skill of sitting still. Just do that. Sit still. Don't tap your feet. Don't pace around. Don't dive into emails. Don't send pestering (verging on desperate) messages. Just sit. This will allow you to recharge, it will allow you to notice what you'd normally miss and it will train you to sit with uncertainty, rather than forcing a poor decision based on insufficient information. All of those things will give you an edge against your competition. And you get to keep your friends. I think that's a pretty big return on investment.

If you recognise yourself in the above and you're a boss or a leader, there is a good chance you've projected the mindset of 'activity is better than productivity' onto your teams. And because you are fabulous and they want to please you, they will feel the pressure to do something, anything, to stay busy. For all the reasons above, this is not doing you or them any favours. If you've been creating this culture in your organisation, then, if you're lucky, your team are underperforming. If you're unlucky, they are getting ready to leave or to crash and burn out. The smartest ones will leave. If you recognise yourself in the above and you're a solopreneur, then it's time to re-think that attitude. If you crash and burn out then you're no good to anyone – least of all your business. Don't let that happen to you. Stick with me. The juice is worth the squeeze.

This barrier is a biggie and you'll see it's covered across almost all of the habits. If this is your biggest barrier, I recommend reading the HABITS chapters in order.

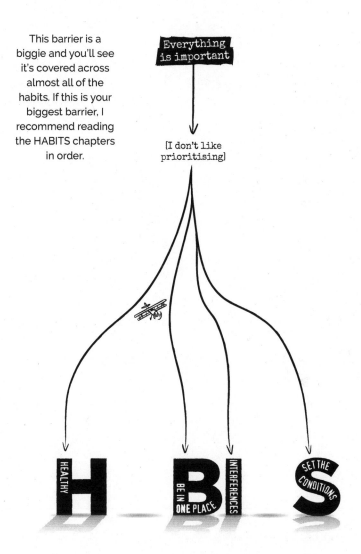

Barrier 3: Everything is important
(I don't like prioritising)

If you are running a business, it's highly likely that you'll be incorporating multiple roles: HR, admin, customers, suppliers. If you run a small business or are a solopreneur, you may even be wearing several of these hats yourself. How do you divide your attention between all of these essential tasks? How do we prioritise when everything is Important? I promise you, no matter how complex or dynamic your job is, uni-tasking is completely possible.

When you're flying an aircraft, there's a lot more to it than just looking out of the window. I had hundreds of data inputs to process: multiple instruments in the cockpit, listening to my crew, listening out for radio calls, making radio calls, preparing weaponry, reacting to the threat environment, reacting to the weather, honouring airspace restrictions, map reading and so on. There's a *lot* going on. It could very easily reduce even the most robust of brains to total goo within seconds. So, we had a work cycle. It might look something like this.

Aviate: 'Fly the aircraft'. Make sure it's flying upright and we're not about to crash into a hill.

When I'm happy the aircraft is flying straight and level, then I'll go to the next task.

Navigate: Where am I going and how will I get there? I'd pick up the map, plot my course, then put the map down.

Back to flying the aircraft. Still upright. Phew. Then I'll go to the next task.

Communicate: Who do I need to speak to next to enable my mission? Who needs to know what I'm doing? (See how you could ask yourself exactly the same question in your business?)

Back to flying the aircraft. Still upright. (Dang, I'm good.) Then I'll go to the next task.

Administrate: Do I need to get some more fuel? Have I updated my GPS setting?

And so on. For flying enthusiasts, within the 'aviate, navigate, communicate, administrate' work cycle, we had subsidiary work cycles: Lookout (make sure we don't hit anything), Attitude (make sure we are the right way up), and Instruments (make sure the speed and height are correct).

Apart from being seriously impressed at how jolly clever I am, I hope I've demonstrated an important point here. I'm *still* focusing on *one* thing at a time. And I'm *choosing* that one thing. If I can uni-task in a helicopter, you can uni-task too. And what's more, it will totally pay off.

Why it's worth overcoming this barrier

In his fabulous book *The Morning Huddle: Powerful customer experience conversations to wake you up, shake you up and win more business!* David Avrin says that if we look at the science of multi-tasking we can draw the following conclusion: divided attention is no match for undivided attention.[8] If you don't prioritise effectively, your employees and/or your customers will know. You'll be distracted by your inbox, another customer, or another task, which means you'll only give your partial attention to someone. And *it's obvious*. It's a very quick way to piss people off and discourage them from doing business with you.

To compound this problem, if you're only giving part of your attention, you're going to miss things. Plus, you'll waste people's time when they have to repeat themselves. This is literally one of the first things Avrin mentions in his book. He is dedicated to first-class customer experience, which includes being super responsive, but even he will concede that most people would prefer to have your undivided attention, even if that means waiting for it. When you give someone your full attention, you're saying, 'You are my top priority.' Nothing says we value our people better than that.

And things *can* often wait. As well as 'Fly the aircraft', we had another phrase we used equally as often, which was, 'Let's talk about this on the ground'. In other words, things would come up that we would deliberately choose to deal with later so that it wouldn't detract from our number one priority task: flying the aircraft.

If we are really honest with ourselves, a lot of the time we tell ourselves we need to be reactive simply because we don't like prioritising. The advantage of having a deliberate work cycle is that it forces us to prioritise (remember we can only focus on *one* thing at time anyway, so might as well pick the most important thing). Rather than being totally reactive and out of control, we are increasing our chance of being proactive and we are managing our attention most effectively.

We'll look at the work cycle in more detail later. For now, please take the point: no matter how reactive you think you need to be (and you need to be prepared to have a good old Paddington stare at your priorities first), it's absolutely possible to uni-task. So, *no* excuses.

This is a common and
significant barrier for many.
Chapters 6 and 8 – Habits I and
S – will deal with this in detail.

Other
people
need me

[I don't
like
saying
no]

INTERFERENCES

SET THE
CONDITIONS
S

Barrier 4: Other people need me
(I don't like saying no)

Hopefully, I've convinced you that you don't always need to
react to your clients, colleagues, boss, etc *immediately*. For reasons
already stated, sometimes it's better to use tactical patience,
but I accept that not everyone has received that memo (or

read this book – time to buy them a copy, perhaps?), so the chances are they are still going to drive a coach and horses through your good intentions to uni-task. This isn't actually their fault. Remember, when we multi-task, we activate the stress response, and a byproduct of that is our brains prioritise *everything* as urgent important. So whatever trivia these people are disrupting your flow with, they almost certainly believe it's more important than whatever you are doing.

We used to call them bubble buts. We'd spend hours planning a mission, preparing the maps and intelligence reports and ensuring the weather was suitable. Then we'd brief the mission, talking through every landing site, every bit of airspace, every task, every risk to the mission. Then we'd get all togged up like Rambo, putting endless layers of safety equipment on, getting our kit together, making sure we'd remembered the sandwiches. Then we'd be about to walk out to the aircraft, pumped up and ready to save lives. Fully in the mission bubble. Then I'd spot someone hovering hopefully in my periphery.

'Ma'am, I know you're in your bubble, but...' (insert some meaningless trivia, usually related to the summer ball committee meeting). At which point I would sigh extravagantly, roll my eyes conveying exactly how inconvenient this interruption was and say, 'Go on then, what is it?' The simple truth is this: everyone is busy dealing with their own shit. *Nobody* really cares about your priorities, so don't expect them to respect your priorities if you don't. This means we need to stand our ground and communicate our priorities clearly and respectfully.

How do we do that without losing our jobs/credibility/cool? How do we say no? Simple. We don't. We say yes. But, we are intentional about to whom, to what and when we say yes. We'll explore bubble buts and the 'intentional yes' in more detail later. For now, it's enough to know that this is a challenge we can definitely manage, even though we don't like feeling indispensable... Which brings me to what is often the real issue here.

I remember meeting a charming business coach at one of those dreadful expos in Excel. It was badly marketed, the organisers had mis-sold the event and ripped people off and so everyone was in a bad mood. Try selling mindfulness in that environment! If someone had advised me to just 'let it go' after wasting £4,000, I'd probably have head-butted them. Having established there was no point going after customers, I figured I might as well chat with fellow sellers, so I spent a very pleasant thirty minutes swapping notes about coaching with a lovely man. What he said next was worth every penny I'd grudgingly spent on the show.

'I'm a compulsive helper,' he declared proudly. If he could have had a badge with that on, I have no doubt he would have. I wanted to pack him up and take him home with me. The reason this comment was so helpful was because it shone a light on the main problem. The truth is, we *like* helping people. It gives us a purpose. We feel a warm glow of self-satisfaction when we are needed, which means that a lot of the time, we don't want people to work it out for themselves – because then they might work out they don't need us. Or even worse. They might work out how to do it better than us, and then we'd be redundant.

The point is, whether we realise it or not (and most of the time we don't), we help others for our own selfish reasons. It has nothing to do with how needy they are. It's to do with how much we need to be needed. The reason I'm pointing this out is so you can understand that it's probably *us* – not others – putting this barrier up, which is not a reason to be hard on ourselves. It's a reason to be relieved. Remember: if we can put those barriers up, we can also take them down.

Why it's worth overcoming this barrier

Here's the thing – our job as leaders is to be replaceable. To nurture and grow those in our team so that they can go on and be better than us. That means that not being needed is a sign of *great* leadership. Equally, as a solopreneur, you probably want to allow your business to scale up and expand and perhaps sell it for zillions of pounds so you can relax on a beach. So, learn to be dispensable and you'll reap the rewards. We'll explore this further later on. Please feel free to be very excited about it. Here are four other advantages to learning how to be a bit more dispensable:

- The first advantage is that we can prioritise our time the way we choose, without being completely at the mercy of others. By doing that we will perform better and, ultimately, serve others better.

- When we stand our ground, we are role-modelling that for others. Just think, 'If it's OK for the boss, then maybe it's OK for me.'

- Perhaps other people might follow our lead and stop running around like headless chickens? That's a great gift we can give others. If you are prepared to be firm but respectful, people might just think twice about needlessly bothering you in the future. So, you've saved them and you time.

- My *favourite* reason: when we don't immediately problem-solve for other people, something magic happens – they work it out for themselves.

Uni-tasking 'under fire' is woven into the fabric of this book, as illustrated here.

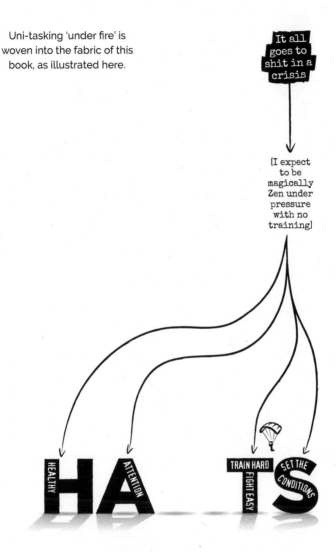

It all goes to shit in a crisis

[I expect to be magically Zen under pressure with no training]

Barrier 5: It all goes to shit in a crisis
(I expect to be magically Zen under pressure with no training)

There's a moment in *Top Gun* when Kelly is interviewing Tom (in my head, we're on first name terms – just go with it). She's quizzing him about his decisions during a dogfighting mission.[9]

'What were you thinking up there?' she asks.

'If you think up there, you're dead,' Tom replies firmly. Apart from the fact that this is one the best moments in cinematic history (so good, in fact, he repeats this line to Rooster in the sequel, *Top Gun: Maverick*),[10] Tom raises an excellent point.

We are not designed to think rationally under pressure. We're designed to react. Quickly. That's why we often come out with words before we've engaged our brains. (If you're like me, these words may contain expletives – I still feel bad about what I said to the DPD man when I was panicking about a recent deadline.) And in order to react quickly under pressure, the amygdala looks to the hippocampus and asks, 'What did we do last time?' And then repeats whatever it did last time. Again. And again. This will happen until an automatic behaviour is learned. That's why we have 'default' responses to stress. It means we don't have to think, we can react really, really fast. ('Don't think, just do,' as Tom went on to explain.) Quite clever of us.

The problem is that if your default response is to clam up (the classic freeze response), run away (flight) or yell at someone (I think the DPD man knows my default response is fight), that's not going to help. Equally, if your default response to stress is to multi-task, you're not going to magically start uni-tasking the next time you're in crisis. This is why, in Habit H, we will look at how to get from the 'freaking out' part of the stress curve to the 'stretch' part, so we actually have a hope of uni-tasking. However, I want to take this to the next level, because I recognise there *will* be times the pressure is on and you can't do much about it. You're not going to have time to do a quick meditation.

How do we uni-task under pressure when our fight or flight response has kicked in? *It has to be an automatic behaviour...* And the easiest way to make something automatic is through repetition. Which means we practise, practise and practise some more. In the military, this is called 'Train hard, fight easy'. You can call it whatever you like. The important thing is you commit to the training. You commit to practising uni-tasking *every day*.

Why it's worth overcoming this barrier

Most of us would prefer not to have to put the hard work in. We'd prefer to be naturally good at everything. But the only thing we are naturally good at is picking the wrong queue in passport control.

Everything else is learned. Everything else we work for. Which, if you look at it another way, means it's all up for grabs. So, commit to the training and then uni-tasking will become automatic. Being a ninja under pressure will be easy and everyone will ask you what your secret is.

Another reason that the juice is worth the squeeze is that most of our competitors won't bother to put the training in. It's the first thing that gets slashed from a budget. It's the first thing we cut from our day when we're feeling overloaded. (Which, ironically, means we will perform less efficiently and, therefore, end up more overloaded – see what I mean about the brain doing the least helpful thing it can under pressure?)

This means you'll have the edge over the competition. Now, I appreciate you don't have the luxury to spend your time training when you need to be making money. Fear not – this book will show you how to train on the job. Because guess what? Every time you uni-task, you'll be more effective in your business *and* you're training your brain at the same time.

So, with all that in mind – let's start training, shall we? Remember: you can refer back to these sections whenever you need a refresh, or skip to the relevant sections below if you have a burning desire to overcome a specific challenge. This is where we're going to dig deep into the HABITS mnemonic, and, because it makes sense, we'll start at the beginning with H.

Key takeaways

- There are myriad reasons we find it hard to uni-task. Go easy on yourself if you've told yourself that you can't do it.

- But don't go *too* easy on yourself. The greatest thing that will get in the way of your stardom is you.

Commitment to action

Hopefully you've already completed the Five Whys exercise to find out how you are getting in your own way. (If not, now's a really good time to do it.) Now it's time to decide to get out of your own way. You don't need to overthink it. Just make a commitment. For example: 'I previously told myself that everything is equally important, but I now see that this is my reluctance to prioritise, which is great news because I can do something about that.' Boom.

PHASE TWO

CHANGE YOUR HABITS

Now it's time to change your habits. I've created the HABITS mnemonic to guide you through this step by step. We bloody loved our mnemonics in the military. Partly because we imagined it made us sound dreadfully clever. But it also made it easy for us to remember processes and use them with a high degree of consistency, even when under pressure. *And* it helped to break a larger mission or task into manageable chunks. In other words, it made seemingly difficult things easy.

3

H Is For Healthy

BOTTOM LINE UP FRONT

Uncomfortable truth:
You are not thriving on stress.
It doesn't make you stronger.

Business gains:
Approach problems with clarity and agency.
Avoid yelling at your colleagues.

Personal gains:
Reduce the likelihood of crashing and burning out. Avoid feeling like a dick when you yell at your colleagues.

Stress is a spectrum

Some people believe that one's character is only truly revealed when you are under pressure. I simply don't agree. Performance under pressure is not as instinctive as we've been led to believe. We are not born with a natural ability to remain ice-cool in a crisis while making a Bond-esque 'glib remark' or 'pithy comeback'. In terms of crisis management, the only thing we are born with is the fight or flight response: our threat system. And it has *one* job. To keep us alive. This means that if our threat system kicks in when we are under pressure, we will do *just about anything* to neutralise that threat, whether it is real or perceived. Which means that under pressure we might show up as a bit of dick. Some people might judge you for that. I won't.

Suffice it to say, if you've been telling yourself you thrive under stress or, more likely, that you *should* be able to thrive under stress, it's time to let yourself off the hook. *No one* is designed to thrive under stress. We are designed to *survive*. That doesn't mean we need to throw our hands in the air and say, 'What's the point? I'm destined to always turn bright red or forget my boss's name or fart nervously when I'm giving a presentation.' Not true at all. Because stress is a spectrum.

Cortisol and its impact on performance

When we refer to stress, what we usually mean is the right-hand part of the curve (see figure) or the unhealthy side of the curve – which is where our cortisol levels are very high. Cortisol, by the way, is an alertness hormone; it's responsible for waking us up in the morning and for jolting us awake when we find ourselves getting sleepy at the wheel and veering towards the rumble strip. Cortisol isn't bad; it's just that when levels get very high, our performance starts to drop off, as shown by the graph. That's because our fight or flight system is now almost entirely running the show and is basically bypassing the more rational part of the brain, so we no longer have the same ability to regulate our emotions, prioritise and problem-solve.[11] In his book *Thinking, Fast and Slow*, this is what Daniel Kahneman refers to as 'system 1' thinking.[12]

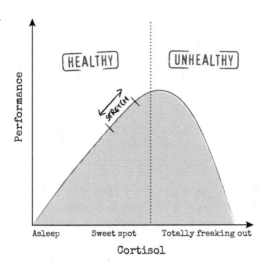

The cortisol curve

In the long term, consistently high levels of cortisol in our system can lead to high blood pressure, reduced immune system, insomnia, reduced libido, reduced appetite, higher blood sugar levels and even diabetes and heart problems.[13] When we are running around all day every day with our hair on fire, thinking that we are killing it, all we are actually doing is killing ourselves. Slowly and painfully. This is why I've called it the *unhealthy* part of the cortisol curve. Hopefully this convinces you that we are not designed to thrive under this much stress. Too much cortisol is a truly pants idea.

But there's more. Do you ever have those days when you never get to the end of your 'to-do' list? In fact, if anything, the list gets bigger. Well, that's probably because you're running around full of cortisol. And when you're full of cortisol, your brain prioritises everything as urgent important so it won't miss any impending threats. The brain will keep all these threats front of mind to make sure you don't get caught out, so your mind ends up going round and round at a million miles an hour. Of course, it's hard to keep track of all these threats, so it's natural to jot them down in a list. Put your hand up if you love a list. In fact, studies show that writing a list tricks your brain into thinking you've completed the tasks and allows you to relax a little.[14] This is fine if your list is manageable, but when you end up with a list that's off the page, the result is that it stresses you out even more – and we already know the negative impact that stress has on our performance and health. So, *more* stress created by endless to-do lists isn't helping us. Being pleasantly busy is good. Being totally maxed out isn't.

Finding a balance

So, what's the answer? Is it to burn the to-do list, give up our high-powered jobs and sit on a beach for the rest of our lives? Well, no. Too little cortisol can be equally problematic.[15] If there were very low cortisol levels, we'd be asleep, which is great at night or if you need to endure long periods of incarceration or boredom (we used to call this the 'horizontal time accelerator'), but in the daytime, low alertness levels mean we are operating in the zombie zone. At work, this will manifest as presenteeism (being there but not present) and will impact your (and your team's) output, commitment to tasks and service to your customers. If you (or they) are operating machinery, it could manifest as accidents and even fatalities. In our personal lives, it could manifest as low energy, apathy and lack of purpose. Shaking things up a bit is helpful for our performance and our wellbeing.

What we really want to do, then, is operate on the optimum part of that spectrum so that we absolutely knock it out of the park and prioritise effectively. This part of the spectrum is often known as 'stretch', which is why people often think that a little bit of stress is good for them.[16] The stretch zone lies just outside our comfort zone and is where the best growth and learning occurs. It is, so long as you are on the left side of the curve. But if you've tipped over into the right-hand side, it's all going to go to shit pretty quickly. So, a crucial first skill to learn is how to *get ourselves* back to the optimum part of the spectrum. The *healthy* part of the spectrum. And to do that, we need to know how to get from fight or flight back to stretch. We do this by activating our parasympathetic nervous system. Excitingly, we have more control over this than we often realise.

To understand how to get ourselves back into stretch, we simply need to understand how the fight or flight response works. First, let's revisit what happens when the fight or flight system (sympathetic nervous system) is triggered: heart rate increases, breathing rate increases, focus increases, muscle tension increases.

CASE STUDY: Flight or flight in action

I can remember a time when this was most embarrassingly obvious.

It was when I was flying the Hawk aircraft. The Hawk, for the uninitiated, is what the Red Arrows fly. You may have seen all nine of them effortlessly and gracefully flying in diamond formation, just inches from each other, at 7 miles a minute. They make it look so easy to fly so close to each other. Let me assure you, it's fucking nails.

I only ever had to fly in formation with one or two other Hawks and I was terrible at it. As soon as we got within a few feet of each other, I'd grip the controls so hard you could see the imprint of them in my palms when I landed (muscle tension increases), my gaze would be absolutely glued to the other aircraft, hardly daring to risk a quick scan of the instruments to make sure I wasn't running out of fuel (focus increases to the point of tunnel vision), and to make matters worse, I'd start hyperventilating. I could just about conceal the first two because my instructor didn't know where I was looking and he couldn't feel my force on the controls, but in the Hawk, we flew with oxygen masks. We could *hear* each other breathe – and I was breathing like I was in labour.

There was no hiding it; I was totally freaking out. Indeed, it proved to be my nemesis and resulted in me being 'chopped' from fast jets and switching to helicopters. I often refer to this as my Cougar moment. You know the guy in Top Gun who falls apart under pressure? Well, that was me. I was a Cougar. (It's OK to chuckle at this. My partner is nine years younger than me and I'm owning it.)

Becoming aware of your combat indicators

Your turn. How do *you* show up when you're on the right-hand side of the curve? You need to think about this so that I can transport you back to the moment where you start to tip over the curve. I want you to experience that moment and describe what it looks like for you. Has someone just changed the plan on you at short notice? Has a customer asked for the moon on a stick? Has someone in your department sent a hastener email? Whatever it is, this is your trigger. Or your 'wires moment'. This is the moment when the proverbial hits the fan and you are most likely to start manically multi-tasking. Reflect on what yours might be. What is your 'wires' moment? (If you prefer, you can call it your Cougar moment.) Next, consider how you think, feel and act in this moment:

- Do you feel yourself tensing up?

- Do you feel frustration or a surge of panic?

- Do you sweat?

- Do you snap at people or do you prefer to hide in the loo?

These reactions are your 'combat indicators' (ie, a sign that your brain has gone into fight or flight mode). Remember, if you've tipped over to the unhealthy side of the curve, you're not going to be capable of rational thought and you might not be the most self-aware at this point (it's a different part of the brain running the show now). It's crucial to reflect on what your indicators are when you're feeling calm and resourced, so that you're more likely to recognise the indicators when you're not calm and resourced. It's about comparing the two.

So, go ahead and write down your combat indicators. Be honest. In the midst of these 'indicators' you will experience an increase in heart rate, blood pressure, breathing, muscle tension and focus. Remember, this is you in fight or flight mode and your brain is doing exactly what it's designed to do in that moment: protect you and keep you alive, even if you end up behaving like a bit of a dick. When I freak out, I usually yell at my child and his big grey-green eyes fill with tears. And then I shout at him again for making me feel bad by looking cute. So, trust me, no matter what your combat indicators are, I'm not judging!

Creating change

There is something really cool about the way we are designed. Experts refer to this as the 'cognitive framework'.[17] What this means is that our thoughts, emotions, behaviour, physiology and the chemicals in our brain are all linked and influence each other. For example, this is why we feel grumpy when we are tired or irritable when we are hungry. It's also why fresh air and exercise are incredibly effective at improving our mood and our disposition to think more positively.

What's brilliant about this is we don't have to try and *will* ourselves to feel calm or try to slow down a hammering heartbeat when we're nervous. We simply have to change something, *anything*, within the cognitive framework and everything else will follow suit. Essentially, we need to find a super-simple way to reduce our cortisol when we are totally freaking out, lest we all want to become Cougars (not the worst outcome if you ask me, but it's always good to keep our options open). Fortunately, there are a few.

How to get from the unhealthy to the healthy part of the curve

Let's begin with the one that's the easiest to influence. For most people, it's the breath. Simply slow down your breathing and, as if by magic, your cortisol levels will start to reduce. Don't get me wrong, you're not going to go from totally freaking out to totally Zen in one breath exhale, but it will take the edge off, and even if that's just by a fraction, you're now moving in the right direction. Well, really you're moving left on the graph, but you get my meaning. The easiest way to slow down your breathing is to exhale for longer than you inhale.

EXERCISE: Reducing your breathing rate

My favourite way to do this is to practise the 'cortisol cool-down' exercise. You may decide to do this while going on a brisk walk to start with; I certainly find it helps to *move* when I'm feeling stressed. Not only does this satisfy our need for 'flight' (so we are working *with* our brains, not against them), but it often removes us from the stressor and reduces the likelihood of us losing our shit at our loved ones or colleagues. Plus, you can feel satisfied for having edged closer to your daily step goal, which brings the additional benefit of exercise (and perhaps a touch of smugness). It's what I like to call a reward multiplier. One action, multiple rewards.

- Start off by walking at whatever pace feels right to you. If it's not convenient or appropriate to walk, this works just as well sitting still.
- Simply start counting your inhale for 4 and counting your exhale for 4.
- Repeat this 4 times.
- Now inhale for 4 and exhale for 6.
- Repeat 4 times.

If you started off walking, you may notice you've slowed down the pace. Your breathing will also have slowed, as will your heart rate and muscle tension. Because of this, your cortisol levels will have reduced.

This exercise is one of the recovery actions you can practise when you feel like you are about to blow your top or dissolve into a puddle of tears. If it doesn't float your boat, there are two more techniques you can use: reducing muscle tension and increasing our focus. Let's start with muscle tension.

EXERCISE: Reducing muscle tension

A popular way to do this is what's called progressive muscle relaxation. Here's a step-by-step summary of the exercise:

- Start at your toes and scrunch them up. Hold for 3 and then relax.
- Then move up to your calves. Repeat.
- Then your thighs. Repeat.
- Now your abdomen. Repeat.
- Continue to move up through your chest, your shoulders, your biceps, forearms and fingers.
- Finish at your neck, your jaw and your whole face.

If it's not appropriate to do the entire exercise, scrunching your toes up repeatedly will have the same effect (and is less likely to scare your colleagues when you're in a meeting with them). Equally, if you find yourself at the wheel of a car, you could clench and unclench the steering wheel (best to do this when stationary or driving in a straight line). Hopefully you get the point: you can adapt this exercise to whatever your situation is.

I found this technique extremely useful when I was flying my helicopter. I'd be hovering in a small clearing in a wood, surrounded by things to bump into so it was particularly critical that I could hold a steady hover. It may strike you as odd that the hardest thing about flying a helicopter, when you start out at least, is staying still. Having gone from screaming around at 480 mph, it defies logic that flying at 0 mph could be the most frightening and stressful exercise, but it often was. It was not unusual to find myself totally clenched up from my toes all the way to my eyes, desperate not to drift into any obstacles.

When you're hovering, you're basically just flying in close formation with the ground and the surrounding obstacles (ie, you do some magic with your hands and feet to make sure the visual markers stay in the same spot in your window). The problem is, the more of a death grip you have on the controls, the harder it is to 'feel' the aircraft and respond to any slight movement. Plus, the more I gripped the controls, the more 'agricultural' my handling was, so I'd end up over-controlling. If any of you reading this are horse riders, you'll know exactly what I mean. A horse, just like a helicopter, feels what you feel. Freaking out is disastrous. Luckily, I discovered a fiendishly simple solution: relax the grip on the controls.

It felt totally counterintuitive to do this, but I realised that all I had to do was deliberately unfurl my toes and relax my shoulders and everything became easier; I felt a lot more in control. Thus, I mastered the hover and, ultimately, formation flying. In fact, I even came top of the class. Miraculous. So, I can attest to how effective the simple action of relaxing your muscle tension can be. Again, it might only be a marginal difference, but in the high-performing world that we all live in, a small margin is all you need.

The final technique is around widening your focus. You may recall from the Hawk example that I was completely fixated on the other aircraft, so for this exercise, I need you to think about a time when you've felt stressed or overwhelmed:

- Did you find it hard to concentrate on anything else?

- When you tried to complete other tasks, did you find your mind drifting back to the stressor in question?

If you did, that's not a deficiency. That's your fight or flight doing its job by keeping the biggest threat in the front of our mind. You see, you're not broken after all! Even better news, this presents another opportunity for us to engage the parasympathetic nervous system and reverse the fight or flight trajectory. We simply need to widen our focus.

EXERCISE: Widening your focus

Think of this as going from tunnel vision to funnel vision. I call this active noticing. Probably the easiest thing to do to initiate that is to *move your head*. In the flying world we called this a lookout scan. Here are some practical ways to apply this:

- If you're in a meeting, look up from your screen, or your notepad. Take in the view. The people around you. Notice their non-verbal cues. Notice the language they are using. Notice, with perhaps some wry humour, if they are sitting in the same seats they sit in every day forever and ever. (We are, after all, creatures of habit, which is why uni-tasking will be much easier for us when we make it a habit – more of that later.)

- If you're stuck in traffic, start to notice the other people sitting in the queue and see if you can work out what music they're listening to by the way they move. Might they listen to the same podcasts or radio stations as you? Might they listen to the same radio stations as you *used* to listen to or may find yourself listening to in the future? Be curious about where they are going. Do they appear to be in work mode, or do you think they are planning a social visit? Have a bit of fun watching your fellow humans as they go about their lives. You might even start to feel a sense of shared humanity. And, therefore, less stressed.

Now let's pull this all together and give you a complete solution that will work in your world.

Deciding your immediate actions

When we were in flying training, we had these things called *immediate actions*.[18] These were the drills we would carry out when the shit hit the fan (or the aircraft hit the wires). There are a few characteristics of immediate actions worthy of note:

- They would be simple actions (like 'Fly the aircraft'). Remember, when we're in fight or flight mode, the rational part of the brain (the pre-frontal cortex) gets bypassed and we are not capable of more complex 'system 2' thinking.

- We would commit these actions to memory. We can thus defer to what is already stored in the memory banks (which is what our brains want to do in the moment anyway) instead of thinking up some novel way of responding in the moment.

- We would practise them repeatedly. The key to doing anything well under pressure is to make it automatic. The way to make something automatic is repetition – we'll revisit this in Habit T (Train hard, Fight easy).

What are *your* immediate actions? What simple action can you take that will help you to feel calmer? Remember, keep it simple. Write it down and commit it to memory. And keep it consistent. Pick *one* tool that you will do every time you start freaking out (choose from the above or add your own).

How to avoid going into the unhealthy part in the first place

Now, this is where we are going to get really clever. You see, the combat indicators are probably a sign you are on the *right-hand* side of the curve. The unhealthy side. But remember I said that the best performance happens in stretch, and remember where that was on the curve? It wasn't at the apex. It was just below the apex, on the healthy side of the curve. So, in fact, the stretch zone we are aiming for isn't the point at which we reach the absolute pinnacle of our performance. It's ever so slightly short of that mark. Why do you think that is?

It's to give us a bit of a buffer. If we get thrown an unexpected curveball, we've got a little bit of capacity in the bag before we tip over the edge and start dribbling. In the military, we used to call it 'a little bit extra for Mum'. For example, when we were calculating how much fuel we needed to complete a certain part of the mission, we'd always round up so that if we had to divert around weather, we would have a reserve. Hence, we'd be more likely to make it home to our mums for tea and medals. We're simple creatures at heart (and mums are brilliant).

We can apply the same principle to operating in stretch. It needs to feel uncomfortable so we perform at our best, but the skill is being just uncomfortable enough – not to the point that you've got nowhere to go when the pressure mounts up a notch. This means we need to learn how to hit that sweet spot and *not to overshoot it.*

🍋 Why the juice is worth the squeeze

Remember those combat indicators? Well, they're a sign that we've overshot, which will happen. And when they do, apply the immediate actions. It's not the end of the world.

But wouldn't it be excellent if we could apply those immediate actions *before* we get to that point? That means we can *stay* in the optimum part of the stress curve and operate on our A game. Which means we will prioritise more effectively and do our best work. And that's great for business. The trick here is to know thyself.

Learning about your early warning indicators

Most of us don't notice we're in panic mode until we've snapped someone's head off, but with practice and by applying friendly curiosity to ourselves, we can start to build a picture of what we look like just after we've been triggered and just before we pass through the point of diminishing returns.

I'm going to call these 'early warning indicators', so I can keep to the military theme (partly for consistency, but mostly because I want you to think I'm cool). Over time, simply by paying attention to your triggers and early warning indicators, you might find you're able to carry out your immediate actions sooner. This ultimately saves you time and energy from having to come back from the right-hand side of the curve, reduces the dip in performance that you would experience from the right-hand side, and hopefully means you yell at your colleagues a little less often.

Now you can attack the to-do list. Being in a good headspace in the optimum part of the curve is the perfect time to sit down and start uni-tasking.

EXERCISE: Identifying your triggers and indicators

Here's an exercise you can do over the next few days to build a picture of your behaviour. Write down your response to each of these questions when you feel triggered and see if you can notice any patterns:

- My triggers (what stresses me out): What happened?
- My early warning indicators (my thoughts): What was I thinking? What was I feeling?
- My combat indicators (how you know when you're stressed out): What physical sensations did I notice? What was my behaviour?

Key takeaways

- Being in the right headspace is crucial to productivity. We need to be in the right part of the stress curve to prioritise effectively.

- We can get there by learning our triggers (what stresses us out), our early warning signs (what we were thinking), our combat indicators (how we know when we're stressed out) and having some immediate actions (simple actions so we can calm the fuck down).

Commitment to action

Start implementing your immediate actions. Remember, the more you practise, the more proactively you can act and catch yourself before you get totally stressed out.

4

A Is For Attention

BOTTOM LINE UP FRONT

Uncomfortable truth:
It is not someone else's fault that
you find it hard to uni-task.

Business gains:
Build resilience against external and
internal distractions so you can focus
for longer and do deep work.

Personal gains:
Stop lying by telling yourself that, 'I am easily
bored or have a short attention span.' Learn to use
your attention as a force for good so you can
ditch the baggage and feel better.

Excuses, excuses

Now you've got yourself into the healthy part of the cortisol curve, you're in the sweet spot. You can attack that to-do list. You sit down to do the first task. But then you remember you haven't had a cup of coffee for ten minutes, so you make a cup. Then you sit back down. You quickly check social media to make sure you're not missing out on any fun. While you're doing that, you remember that you *need* to buy some drain unblocker. You buy the drain unblocker. You can finally start your work. And just as you're getting into it, an alert pops up from a colleague in the chat: 'Just checking you got my email.' This is the point when you might sigh and say, 'Why can't I just have a minute of peace to do my work?' Never mind all the previous tricks your mind has played on you. That's forgotten. It's someone else's fault.

Do you recognise yourself in this? Go on, it's OK. I am brilliant at finding external causes for my distractibility. Just ask my partner what happens when he creeps past me on his way out the door and 'disturbs my flow'. (Actually, don't ask him; you might think less of me.) I'll give you my own PG version. I spend about ten minutes getting really cross that he's bursting my bubble and feel all sorry for myself that I'm cross and, therefore, too upset to work. I might even make a mental note of how much time this has cost me so I can point it out to him later. (The unrated version contains expletives, in case you're worried about where this was going.) Now, who's the one that's stopping me from uni-tasking after he's left the house? Not him. Me and my own stubbornness. In other words, it's not the distraction that is impacting my productivity. It's my response to the distraction that's impacting my productivity. I understand how easy it is to be sucked into our circle of concern and find comfort in the fact that our lack of uni-tasking is someone else's fault, but no matter how comforting it may be, it just isn't helping us.

If we want to change our work habits and start uni-tasking, we have to take control of our behaviours. Not only will that make us more productive, but in my case, it also makes me more bearable to live with. That's why I asked you to do the Five

Whys exercise earlier and to make sure you used I-language. If you did the exercise, you may also have realised that your own mind is often working against you, and hopefully, you will recall that this is not your fault. Our brains are designed to be distractable so we can detect emerging threats.

EXERCISE: Just breathing

Set a timer for one minute and focus on your breathing. Nothing else – just your breathing. Notice your in-breath. Notice your out-breath. That's it.

Any time you get distracted – maybe you've started thinking about the exercise or that to-do list or maybe you heard a noise and started to listen in to that – just take note of it without giving yourself a hard time and bring your attention back to your breathing.

How often did you get distracted in a minute? More than once? More than three times? According to a report by the Centre For Attention Studies at King's College London, it's not uncommon for us to get distracted after just a matter of seconds.[19] A report by Microsoft concluded that our attention now typically hovers around eight seconds, which appears to be shorter than twenty years ago.[20] So, it could be tempting to blame that all on technology (or, in my case, my partner), but it's important we acknowledge the simple fact that the brain likes to wander.

Thinking is hard, but it's worth the effort

Concentrating is *hard work*. It takes effort, and we are wired to conserve energy where we can. So, if we don't have to expend effort, we won't. That's why it can be hard to get into difficult tasks and why we tend to procrastinate. (You have no idea how many cafes I searched before deciding I'd found the 'perfect spot' to write this chapter. I'm not ruling out moving before writing the next paragraph.)

It's also why we tend to operate on autopilot a lot of the time. In other words, we often delegate our choices to the subconscious. How many times do you reflexively buy the same brand of toothpaste or sit in the same seat on the tube? If we can avoid making deliberate choices, not only is it less effort, but it's also less scary. If we make our own choices, then we have to face the terrifying possibility that we may make a bad choice, and who else would we have to blame but ourselves? This is a hideous prospect. The result is that our factory setting is to give our choices away.

For all these reasons, it's important not to be too hard on ourselves – or anyone else, for that matter. However, if we want to take control of our working habits then we need to start exercising choice where we can. No matter how difficult or scary it may seem. The trick is not to focus on the choices we don't have. There is no point wishing for a world without distractions. It's never going to happen, and even if it did, it turns out that our own minds are against us. The trick is to focus on the choices we *do* have. I can't guarantee that my partner won't disturb my flow on his way out to work, but I *can* choose what to do about it. I can focus on sulking about it. Or I can refocus my attention on the task at hand.

The trick is to learn to refocus our attention where we want it to be once we notice we've become distracted. The beauty and the bummer of it is, it's our choice, and the buck stops with us. Remember, though, that the brain is completely trainable. Every time we refocus our attention where we choose to, we are training our brains. We are building those mindfulness muscles that will help us to maintain and build focus. And we are training ourselves to exercise choice. It's exciting and incredibly empowering. Here is an exercise you can do that will help build those muscles.

EXERCISE: Three-minute meditation

- Sit with an alert but relaxed posture, eyes closed or gaze lowered.

- For the first minute, just allow yourself to check in with what's going on in your mind right now. Do you notice a busy quality or a sense of ease? What thoughts and feelings are around? There's no need to judge them or get involved in a conversation. Don't label them as good or bad. See if it's possible just to observe those thoughts and feelings with friendly curiosity or perhaps even humour.

- For the next minute, narrow your focus to your breath, just focusing on each in-breath and each out-breath, just taking this moment. You have nothing else to do, simply focus on your breath.

- For the last minute, widen your focus to your body. Imagine breathing into your whole body now, nourishing it with each breath. See if you notice any tension anywhere in particular. Imagine breathing into that part of the body now and then, letting go of that tension as you exhale.

- Now, start to become aware of your contact with the outside world. Feel your feet on the floor. If you've done this exercise at your desk, you might become aware of your contact with your hands on the keyboard, readying yourself for whatever is next.

- When you're ready, you can open your eyes and decide where you are going to focus your attention.

The purpose of this meditation is to start in the same place you're likely to be when you get distracted from uni-tasking (ie, in your own head), and then to consciously move focus away from those thoughts and into a singular point – your breathing – and then back out to the outside world, readying you to take on your next task. Practise this anytime you get distracted. Even better, make a habit of practising it regularly so that you can build those mindfulness muscles. It could be when you wake up or immediately before you start work. The more often you practise it, the easier it will be to refocus your attention when you get distracted.

If you're short on time, you can reduce each section to thirty seconds, or you can simply carry out the minute of breathing (ie, the middle minute). You can do this at your desk. You can even do this on the loo, so it really doesn't need to take any extra time out of your day. The point isn't *how long* you do it for; it's how *often* you do it. Do it every day. It will pay off.

Putting it into practice in the moment: The hook

Remember what happened when I hit the wires? I started daydreaming about death. Was that helping me at that moment? No. Remember, distractions will happen. It's not the distraction that matters here. It's how we respond to it. The exercise above helps us to build refocusing muscles, but there's something else I want to add. Something so simple, yet so easy to overlook. It comes down to remembering we have a choice. A lot of the time, when we get side-tracked by unhelpful thoughts, it's simply because we forget we had a choice in the first place. So, it's not so much about flexing those refocusing muscles as it is about remembering, in the moment, that we have the option to use them at all.

To do this, we need a way of reminding ourselves that we have a choice as to where we focus our attention. We need a way of bringing ourselves back into the moment. We need a hook. Mine was 'Fly the aircraft'. Simple, but effective. What's yours? Jot some ideas down. What you're looking to create is a short statement you can say to remind you that where you focus your attention is *your* choice, and now it's time to focus it where *you* want it to be. Your hook is your invitation to flex those refocusing muscles.

Why the juice is worth the squeeze

Remember, there is *one* choice nobody can ever take away from us – and that's where we focus our attention. No matter how many things are competing for a slice of it, nobody can get in our heads and tell us where to focus our attention. It's all about taking back ownership of our attention and focusing it where *we* want it to be.

The benefits of this are twofold. It improves our ability to focus our full attention on our high-value tasks (ie, it improves our ability to uni-task). But it also means we can use our attention as a force for good. In other words, it means we can decide to focus our attention somewhere that is helpful and nurturing for us.

Negative thoughts

Let's revisit the moment when my partner creeps out of the house and disturbs my flow. I admitted to you that I have often been guilty of sulking at this stage. I have a narrative that goes around my head something like this, 'I asked what time he was leaving so that I could make sure I uni-task at a time I won't be disturbed, but then he was late leaving, and that has impacted on me. I think I've made it really obvious how important this task is to me. He obviously doesn't really care, and it doesn't matter what I say because he'll just distract me anyway.' You see, this thirty-second disruption has now become about my own worth to my partner. And now I'm off, finding lots of other evidence that he doesn't really take me seriously. Ten, twenty, even thirty minutes can fly by, I can tell you. When you build up that kind of self-sabotaging momentum, it can be very hard to let it go and regain the state of mind to carry out meaningful work.

As I said before, it's not the distraction that impacts our productivity; it's how we respond to it. But productivity is not the only factor impacted; my response also impacts my mood, sense of wellbeing, self-esteem and relationship. Why do we do it to ourselves? Well, because we are wired for survival. We are wired to look for threats. Which means we are wired to look for the negative – both in ourselves and others. In fact, we have around five negative thoughts for every one positive thought.[21] So, it's not surprising that if we let our thoughts wander mindlessly, they'll often take us down an unpleasant path. And what's sad about that is people will often say, 'Well, if I'm thinking it, there must be some truth in it.' This leads to us having a perverse urge to keep feeding the thought and find some truth that we need to confront about ourselves. It's simply not necessary.

Let me put you out of your misery. If you find yourself falling prey to critical or self-sabotaging thoughts, it is not a sign that you are stupid, worthless or broken. It's certainly not a sign that you need to leave your relationship. It is simply a sign that you're a human being with a normal human brain that is trying to protect you by preparing you for the worst possible outcome. It is a sign that your brain is doing exactly what it is designed to do. Welcome to being human.

But here's the good news. Remember: the brain is completely trainable. And we cannot multi-task: our attention can only be in *one* place at a time. All we have to do is train ourselves to focus our attention somewhere that is helpful, and because we cannot multi-task, we can no longer focus on our critical or self-sabotaging thoughts. Any time we find our mind wandering off in unhelpful directions again, we simply re-focus our attention somewhere helpful.

Noticing and focusing

I call this the dance between *noticing* and *focusing*. Notice where your attention has gone. If it's not helping you, then give yourself permission to focus your attention on something else. And repeat. You'll see I've used the word 'permission' here. That's deliberate. As I mentioned above, we often worry that there is 'no smoke without fire', so if we're thinking something deleterious about ourselves (or others, for that matter), we believe there must be a kernel of truth in it. It's kind of an extrapolated and unhelpful version of 'I think, therefore I am.'

The hardest struggle I've had in life is letting myself off the hook and accepting that, 'I think; therefore, I think negatively, let it go and move on.' I understand how hard it can be to let yourself believe that you don't deserve to think the things that you think. But trust me, you don't. You're brilliant. Notice your thought and then let it go and focus on something that serves you, for example:

• Your chosen work task

• Your breathing

• Recalling something you are grateful for

• Stopping to appreciate a beautiful sunset

In fact, I suggest you write down all the ways you can use your attention as a force for good to have at hand when you need it.

Allow me to introduce you to Winefulness, another exercise you can do to practise the dance between noticing and focusing and using your attention as a force for good. I hit upon the idea of Winefulness when I was training as a mindfulness coach and was learning the 'raisin meditation'.[22] The raisin meditation allows you to practise informal mindfulness by using each sense to experience the raisin. I'd noticed, being a lover of wine and having visited many wine regions, that wine tasting follows a very similar format to a raisin meditation. And I thought, 'Boom! Why not practise mindfulness while doing the things you love!'

The point is you can do this exercise with any food or drink. The idea is that it's enjoyable and it gives you a break from thinking about work, because all work and no play is boring and one of the key components of high performance is recovery.[23]

EXERCISE: Winefulness

· Fetch a glass of your favourite beverage (mine is usually a French red, but the choice is entirely yours).

· Take a moment to notice how it looks in the glass. How does the light reflect off it? How does it move when you tilt the glass?

· If you notice you've started thinking about work, the future or the past, you can just smile at this point ('Ah, there goes my wonderful busy brain again') and then bring your attention back to your beverage.

· Now smell it. What do you notice? How does your nose and mouth respond? If you are making judgements about what the drink will taste like, or perhaps those thoughts about work have returned again, smile and then bring your attention back to your beverage.

· Now drink it. See if you can notice every tiny drop in your mouth. How it feels as you taste it. How your body responds. Become aware of any tendency to immediately have another sip (no judgement here).

· Did you get distracted by thoughts at any point? Worrying about the future? Planning? Ruminating over a past conversation? Overthinking? That's fine. That's what brains do. No need to beat yourself up over it. Just notice it, and then when you're ready, let that thought go and bring your attention back to your beverage.

· And repeat.

Remember, the brain is completely trainable and every time you bring your attention back to where you want it to be, you are building your mindfulness muscles. You can use your hook, in the moment, to remind you to use your mindfulness muscles. Keep practising and you'll find that, over time, it becomes easier and easier to use your attention as a force for good.

Key takeaways

- We are designed to be easily distracted, so it's pointless hoping for a world without distraction. Our own brains will distract us.

- Fortunately, we can train our brains to focus our attention where we choose.

- We can also use a hook to remind us we have a choice and to flex those mindfulness muscles.

Commitment to action

Every day for the next week, practise the three-minute meditation, and then keep going. For the weekend, you can substitute it with the Winefulness meditation.

5

B Is For Be In One Place

BOTTOM LINE UP FRONT

Uncomfortable truth:
Not all tasks are created equal – some are more
important than others. Busy is not a sign of
productivity or importance. It's a sign of a
lack of willingness to prioritise.

Business gains:
Increase efficiency and effectiveness, more time to focus
on higher return projects, create headspace to think
strategically and make more money.

Personal gains:
Create some time in the diary for things
(and people) you love.

Prioritising

Let's start with a reminder: a lot of us find it hard to uni-
task because we don't like or don't feel confident prioritising.
The brain will default to prioritising everything as urgent and
important 'to be on the safe side'. This is a false economy
because it just adds to our stress and reduces our ability to
prioritise. We need an effective system to prioritise our tasks

so that we can do them one at a time. The aim of the matrix is to identify your *important* tasks because these are the ones you'll actually do yourself (others you can delegate, outsource or discard).

Everyone is capable of this and it *will* get easier the more you do it. Let's go back to the to-do list. You're feeling a bit calmer now and you've had a look at the list and realised there are a few things that don't really need to be on it. Great! Funny how when we are feeling less stressed a lot of things seem less urgent. That's a good thing. Go ahead and take them off the list.

This time, when you sit down to make a start, you know that your mind is going to play tricks on you and distract you, but you're ready for it. You've got a killer hook, so any time you get distracted, you can simply refocus your attention on the task at hand. But wait. You've got seven tasks on the list. Which one do you do first? Which one can wait? Ooh, it's so tricky. They *all* seem so important. It's almost like we feel bad if we pick one in case the others get FOMO. What if we pick the wrong one to focus on and accidentally ignore the most important task in the world, ever? What if that one could have had a life-changing impact on our business? No, that feels a bit too risky. Perhaps it's better just to nibble away at a few simultaneously. And then, bam! We're multi-tasking again.

This, in my opinion (I would say humble, but pilots aren't renowned for being humble, and I'd rather just be honest with you because you seem really cool), is the *biggest* barrier that gets in the way of us multi-tasking. Remember what I said before: it's useful to remember that the biggest barriers to our success are actually the ones we put up *ourselves*, not the ones that are created by others or our environment. Well, this could not be truer in this instance. Because the nub of it is this – *we don't like prioritising*.

And yes, we could try blaming technology again for creating an unsustainable expectation on us to respond immediately to everything (*still* mad at the person who invented the two blue ticks on WhatsApp). But remember, blaming the things in our circle of concern might be comforting, but it doesn't get us very far, which means we need to rid ourselves of a couple of limiting beliefs and face the truth.

Busy does *not* equal productive. Busy does *not* equal important. If you did the Five Whys exercise and started with 'everything is important', you may have arrived at this unsettling but necessary conclusion: we feel like we are the big dogs if we're busy. And that's OK; I fell for the lie once, too. Most successful people in our position did. Let's face it: we didn't get to where we are by saying, 'No, I can't do that.' But if you find yourself uttering the words, 'I'm just so busy,' that is not a sign you are more important than the recipient of this news. It just means you've failed to prioritise.

How to prioritise

What follows in this section is a way to address the above challenge, because it *is* hard to prioritise. In fact, I put this out to a poll to find out people's preferred way to prioritise. The results were inconclusive, which tells me this: most of us are making this up as we go along.

First, every time from now until forever, I want you to replace: 'I'm just so busy,' with: 'I'm finding it hard to prioritise.' I promise you, it will change your life. I've also designed a system that you can use to help you prioritise your to-do list.

Decide what's genuinely Important (high-value)

OK, so I love a matrix. If you like lists, then you may want to stick with a list. You may feel some apprehension about switching to a matrix, but think about this: a matrix is really a way of making lists *within* lists. I can prove it to you. Here is the first, which is based on the Eisenhower Matrix for prioritising tasks.[24]

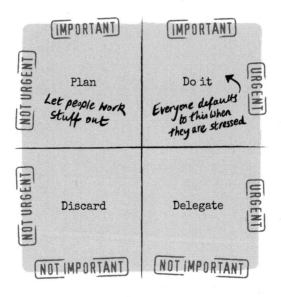

The Urgent–Important Matrix

Start by writing out all your tasks for the week (ie, those that would normally appear on your to-do list). If you have Post-it notes that fit into quadrants of the matrix, you can write your tasks on the Post-it notes. This will make it easier later. Write one task per Post-it note. Next, decide which quadrant you are going to put each task into:

- Urgent/important

- Non-urgent/important

- Urgent/non-important

- Non-urgent/non-important

Look at all the tasks which are *above* the line. These are your important tasks – the ones you will do. Take these and put them in priority order of importance. You don't need to overthink this. You're brilliant and smart and capable, or else you wouldn't be reading this book, so whatever feels right is probably just that. Right. Or it's certainly more right than wrong. Go with your gut and assign your Important tasks in terms of priority (1 being the highest priority). The purpose of doing this is twofold: it makes it easier to do *one* thing at a time if you organise your tasks in priority order and the act of prioritising gets easier and less scary the more you do it. So, this process is just as important as the scores on the doors. There are two types of tasks here:

1. **Urgent important:** These tasks are ones I tend to attack as soon as I have an available moment. Notice: I'm not saying that I attack these tasks *immediately* at the expense of all others. In my experience, even important tasks can wait until you've finished what you were doing – most tasks that are important are *not* life-threatening, so please do yourself a favour and keep some perspective here (I'll expand on this shortly).

2. **Non-urgent important:** These tasks are the ones I schedule to make sure they get done and are not sacrificed to urgent non-important tasks.

Now look at all the tasks which are *below* the line. These also fall into two types:

3. **Urgent non-important:** These tasks are not important, so they are either not the most effective use of your time (so delegate or outsource), or they're not the most effective use of anyone's time (discard).

4. **Non-urgent non-important:** Have you put any tasks in the discard box? If you find it more palatable, you could call this the 'back burner' box, it's entirely up to you. If you haven't, that's OK. I know it's hard. Many of us love a list. And we love being busy (or we think we do). What's more, our mischievous little minds love to play tricks on us: if we think something is important, we often unwittingly assign it as urgent, too. Or if we think something is urgent, we immediately assume it's important. It's not hard to see why we might emphatically declare that *everything* is important. I encourage you, though, to keep an open mind about this. Then, when you're feeling calm and confident, have another look and see if there's anything that could go in the discard box.

Fall out of love with your to-do list

Here's a Jedi mind trick you can try that might help you to increase your 'discard' tasks. Imagine, instead of it being your to-do list, it's someone else's. You know the feeling when someone is hounding you because something is terribly urgent and important to them, and they can't understand why it isn't equally urgent and important to you, too? Newsflash... We don't all have the same tasks in our urgent important box. And therein lies an opportunity. Imagine someone else gave you *their* weekly tasks, and you had to prioritise them. You might find you're less attached to them than they are, and you're more willing to downgrade either their importance or their urgency. Suddenly, you've got a bit of capacity and clarity back. Boom!

Rather than engaging with your to-do list, step back and become an observer. How would you prioritise the tasks if they were on someone else's list? Remember, the more meticulously you prioritise, the more time and energy you can give to your high-value tasks. Discarding a task isn't an act of negligence; it's an act of diligence and courage. If this still doesn't convince you, let me share a piece of wisdom I heard from my friend, Jo Ritchie. She said, 'Everything is important until you get a last-minute offer to see Harry Styles. Then, suddenly you realise which tasks you can drop to make space in your day.' The point is this. We don't *like* dropping things, but it doesn't mean we *can't* drop things. So, see if you can choose just one task that goes in the discard box.

When to do your important tasks

Now it's time to move on to the second matrix. It's natural to assume that we should attack the most important tasks *first* and work through them in priority order, but some important tasks are harder than others, and some tasks, while they may be important to us, may have less impact than others, which is where we need to consider impact vs energy.

In this next matrix, you'll take all the important tasks (the ones *above* the line in the Urgent–Important Matrix) and decide which ones are your *uni-tasks* (the ones in the top-right of the Impact–Energy Matrix).

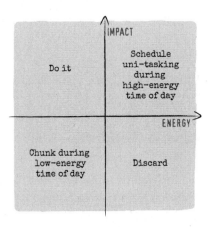

The Impact–Energy matrix

Impact

This is the first axis. To be efficient and effective at work it helps to understand which tasks have the highest impact in relation to your desired outcomes. Of course, only *you* can decide what your desired outcomes are. It might be revenue or profit. It might be making the world safer or cleaner. It might be finishing a certain project. It could be a desired outcome for your top client, because clients love it when we make it about them, and ultimately, a good outcome for them usually ends up being a good outcome for us. (Of course, that's not true if a good outcome for them is for you to give up any work-life balance and become hostage to their every whim. We'll revisit how we deal with the diva high-maintenance clients later on.) If you'd like some assistance with identifying your outcomes, take a few minutes to do the exercise below.

EXERCISE: How to set goals

You can apply the principles of uni-tasking without goals, but ultimately, you'll have more impact if you can work out what your desired outcomes and goals are. Spend a few moments thinking about:

- Your desired outcomes in 3 months
- Your desired outcomes in 1 month
  (which will enable your desired outcome in 3 months)
- Your desired outcomes in 1 week
  (which will enable your desired outcomes in 1 month)

Your answers give you your weekly, monthly and quarterly goals, which will assist in any task-prioritising work you do.

Once you've worked out your desired (business) outcomes (eg, increasing revenue or profit), then the tasks that make the most *meaningful progress towards* your desired outcomes are the highest-impact tasks. Again, my tip here is not to overthink this. Overthinking is the enemy of prioritisation. The trick is to go with your gut. You can test and adjust as you go.

Energy

This is the second axis. Here, you need to identify which tasks are high-energy tasks. For example, I make a living from delivering keynote speeches. I know that for design and preparation work, I need to be on my A game; otherwise, the temptation is I'll cut corners and just copy and paste my previous speech. (Remember, the client loves it when you make it about them, which means tailoring your speech to their desired outcomes.)

Don't forget, this book is also about giving your most spectacular performance – because who wants to be mediocre? So, we need to identify our high-energy, high-impact tasks and dedicate our full attention to them. In other words, our high-impact, high-energy tasks are the ones that we are going to uni-task.

Yes, you read that right. We are singling out which tasks to uni-task. Now, before you panic, I am a realist. I don't expect you to uni-task all day. Don't get me wrong, I love uni-tasking. It's the best thing ever. But even I don't uni-task all day, every day. This is for several reasons:

- It's not practical. Few of us have the ability to shut ourselves off from civilisation and work monastically.

- It's hard work (remember, giving your full attention takes effort), so it can wear us out.

- It's not always necessary. Not all tasks are created equal (which is why it's possible to prioritise). Some tasks have less impact on your desired outcomes, and some are slightly easier on the brain to carry out, such as data entry or deleting emails from cold callers.

- Finally, because we are social animals, we thrive off human connection. So even if, like me, you could happily shut yourself away all day in flow, hammering away at the laptop (truth time – I'm writing this in my pyjamas at 2pm because I woke up feeling inspired and got completely carried away), it's good for us to take a break and engage with other humans – and put proper clothes on.

Establishing your battle rhythm

Have you fine-tuned your list of important tasks based on which have the highest impact on your business? Good. Now, you're going to design your daily and weekly battle rhythm. This is an alignment exercise that will help you take control of your day and turn you into a productivity Jedi.

Attacking high-energy tasks

Often, when we talk about productivity, we talk about time management, but I think the trick to maximising productivity is less about time management and more about attention and energy management.

Now that you've decided which are your high-impact, high-energy tasks, you need to match those tasks to your high-energy time of day so that you can give them your full attention. Because guess what? We tend to pay more attention and achieve deeper focus for longer at high-energy times of day.

For many people, the high-energy time of day is in the morning, because they've been recharged by a night's sleep. Some jump out of bed full of inspiration and want to dive straight into meaty tasks and get them smashed out of the park first thing. Others, though, like to make a coffee, chat with people, or clear out the inbox first. They need a little bit of time to warm up so that they feel ready to take on the high-impact, high-energy tasks (but not so much time that they end up wasting the whole day on filler tasks – feel free to nod wryly if this reminds you of anyone). Others are night owls and they do their best work at 9pm when the kids are in bed and the inbox has stopped blinking at them. (By the way, you can turn those notifications off and achieve this at any time of day. Just saying.) So, take a minute to work out when your *high-energy* time of day is.

Also bear in mind that our motivation and focus will wane as our energy depletes throughout the day. In their book *The One Thing: The surprisingly simple truth behind extraordinary results*, Gary Keller and Jay Papasan refer to this as a 'fuel tank' that gets drained, evidenced by the relationship between the leniency of parole sentences and the amount of time since the judge's last break.[25] The authors analysed lots of factors that might influence a judge's decision to grant parole and found that something as simple as the time of day was one of the most influential factors. Judges tended to default to the decision of 'no parole' as the day wore on and their fuel tanks got low.

This exposes something important in terms of motivation. We often tell ourselves that we just have to be more disciplined. That's rubbish. Discipline (and motivation) is a resource which varies throughout the day. Making decisions and doing deep work *will* drain that fuel tank, so instead of giving ourselves a hard time for having insufficient discipline, we can be clever about how we maximise those periods of high discipline. Of course, we can top up the fuel tank, which is why we often have a late afternoon burst of creativity.

This can happen for several reasons. The most obvious reason has to do with our circadian rhythm. (It's thought our ancestors used to snooze at the hottest time of day and then wake up feeling revived and ready for the hunt. It's also why we typically feel sleepy after lunch.) It could also be because we've been revived after an afternoon walk around the block.

Maybe it's because of the ground rush that creeps in at the end of the day to get stuff done. The point is that you'll probably have more than one high-energy time of day, and it's worth paying attention to when these periods occur. Because not all important tasks are created equal; some tasks require more energy to complete than others, so to get the most out of your magnificent brain, it is a good practice to actively manage your battle rhythm according to your energy levels. In other words, programme your high-energy tasks for your high-energy time of day.

Attacking low-energy tasks

When you are at a lower-energy time of day, this is a good opportunity to address your lower-energy tasks. For most people, low-energy tasks are admin-type tasks. Tim Ferriss recommends a technique called 'chunking' in his book *The 4-Hour Work Week: Escape the 9–5, live anywhere and join the new rich*.[26] This is where you might programme a one- to two-hour block in your day to do two or three of the less fun, but necessary menial tasks.

Nick Wealthall from Yellow Door recommends 'touching things once'.[27] For example, when you see an email pop up, either deal with it straight away or flag it for later without opening it. If you start reading the email, your brain automatically begins working on the response, so by the time you get to write it down, you've already done it once, so you're duplicating your efforts. And because of this attention inertia, it also takes a while for you to refocus on your next task.

CASE STUDY: Attention inertia

A stark example of this was illustrated by a case study we used to examine during our flying training. A young fighter pilot was about to go on a practice air-to-air intercept mission. Just before the pilot walked to the aircraft, his boss asked him to come to the office to see him after the mission. There had been an accusation that the young pilot was making fraudulent expense claims. The pilot flew the mission and several intercepts. After about twenty minutes, the navigator suggested they fly back as he felt it was no longer safe to continue with the mission. On the ground, the navigator asked the pilot what on earth was going on during that flight. The pilot could not recall any of his actions during the mission.[28]

This is an extreme example to show the dangers of our minds being diverted from the task at hand, but the point is that no matter how insignificant it may seem to engage with another task, the momentary refocus can cost us. The less we engage with the distraction, the less it will impact our focus.

By chunking lower-energy tasks into one, you can leave these alone until you are in the right headspace to do them. Then, you don't waste energy doing menial tasks twice and you get the satisfaction of ticking a few things off the list. I also recommend rewarding yourself with a treat after you've done less enjoyable chunking tasks.

Which brings me to my next point. We can also use low-energy time to go for a walk, have a tea break and catch up with friends. This doubles up as a great little treat for doing your tax return as part of your 'chunking'. The bonus is that often, these activities actually *restore* energy levels, which means you are ready to attack your second round of high-energy tasks with a topped-up fuel tank and renewed enthusiasm.

For this reason, I usually plan my meetings in the afternoon from 2pm onwards. I know my energy will be a bit lower, but being an extrovert, I actually gain energy from talking to people. So, this is the time for me to take myself out of uni-tasking isolation and connect with people. I find I leave these meetings buoyed up and raring to attack my next high-value task. So, to recap:

- Attack tasks once.

- Chunk lower-energy menial tasks into one time of day.

- Reward yourself for completing these less enjoyable tasks.

- Take breaks or engage in lower-energy tasks that *restore*.

How long should I uni-task for?

From now until forever, I recommend scheduling 'Uni-tasking' time in your diary for your high-energy time(s) of day and keeping these appointments as if they were appointments with your VVIP client, Harry Styles (or whoever your celebrity crush is).

How long should these blocks of uni-tasking last for, you might ask? There are loads of different statistics out there about how long you should (and can) focus for and they are all worthy of consideration; however, this book is about getting you *started* on the right track, so my recommendation is to *start* with this: Schedule an hour. Aim for twenty minutes.

This is the final thing to note about attention management: concentrating is hard work, so be prepared for the fact that your brain may resist you even if you are in a high-energy time of day. You may procrastinate and piddle about with other things. So, here I'm going to use what I call the 'twenty-minute rule'.[29] In most cases, if you give something twenty minutes, you'll have worked through the kinks (this is true for other people and will come up later when I talk about interferences). I suggest that you give yourself an hour window to achieve twenty minutes of deep work. Twenty minutes is palatable for most of us, so it's easier to make a mental commitment to this chunk of time. That said, for the first ten minutes, it might feel quite hard going. You'll find yourself easily distracted. Push through it. I call this 'pushing through the procrastination barrier'. By twenty minutes, you're probably in flow. And you may just find you end up doing forty-five minutes and you haven't even noticed where the time has gone.

If you're panicking at this stage and thinking, 'But what about the other important tasks that I can't get to during that time?' remember what I said: in my experience, even important tasks can wait until you've finished what you were doing. Because here's the thing: at some point, your attention *will* start to wander again. For me, it's usually the forty-five-minute mark. As long as I've done more than twenty minutes of deep work by this stage, I find it's easier to listen to what my brain is telling me and give it a rest.

This is the point I will turn my attention to my high-impact low-energy tasks. Also known as the 'quick wins'. *This* is the point I will scan my email and respond to the most important ones. Remember the tip of 'touch things once'. I will deal with the important emails *in full*, and the less important ones

I will flag to catch up on during my low-impact low-energy time of day.

By doing this, we are being much more intentional about how we manage our attention. Cal Newport refers to this mindset shift in his brilliant book *Deep Work: Rules for focused success in a distracted world*. Rather than being in a state of near-constant distraction with occasional stints of focus, we are engaged in periods of focus where we occasionally (and intentionally) give in to distraction.[30]

I'm a solopreneur. I do not employ a virtual assistant (VA) to do my email admin. I answer all my emails directly because it doesn't currently suit my needs to outsource my selling. In other words, I want to be the one developing my relationships with my prospects and clients on a one-to-one basis. I'm also a religious uni-tasker. I religiously uni-task from 10 am to 12 pm every day. During that time, I receive no phone calls. I get no email notifications (we'll look at how to set up our environment in the Train Hard, Fight Easy section). I answer new enquiries and follow up enquiries either before 10 am or after 12 pm *or* when I've got a natural break in focus (usually around forty-five minutes). In other words, the longest anybody has to wait for a reply is two hours, but it's usually less than an hour. Time and time again, I get this response: 'Thank you for your speedy reply.' Please keep the faith. Remember what I said right at the beginning. This shit works.

Balancing your weekly battle rhythm with your weekly energy levels

There is one last thing to consider with reference to our battle rhythm, and that's our weekly energy levels. Remember that I said the fuel tank gets drained? We can recharge it on a daily basis by taking some fresh air, having a good old gossip about our celebrity crushes with work colleagues and, of course, having a decent night's sleep, but even then, the fuel tank will start running a bit dry towards the end of the week. This is why we need weekends and holidays. If you're starting up a new business or you're a workaholic, you might say, 'Ha! Weekends are for civvies!' I hear you. I suspect if I didn't live so close to a wine bar, I'd literally never stop working because, well, I kind of love working.

But no matter how much we love our jobs, we cannot give our best performance 365 days a year. Being brilliant is *tiring*. This is why world-class athletes, personal trainers and all sensible people in the world do *not skip* recovery periods. Recovery is utterly indispensable in the arena of high performance. There are two key points to always bear in mind here: know thyself and manage thyself.

Know thyself

We've already explored combat indicators for acute stress in Chapter 3 (too much cortisol), but the combat indicators for sustained 'healthy' levels of cortisol may creep up on you more insidiously. It's worth paying attention to your combat indicators, and even better, your early warning indicators for when the tank is running low. Here are some of mine:

- The bold move I'd been excited to make in my business now seems exhausting and pointless.

- I go to the office to do an important task, and by the time I've got there, I've forgotten what it was.

- When clients present unique challenges for me to solve, I silently swear at my emails as opposed to thinking, 'Ooh, this sounds really interesting.'

- It hurts my brain to think, and I only feel capable of doom-scrolling on Instagram.

- I forget my partner's name (usually mid-bollocking) or accidentally call him by the name of my ex-husband/son/childhood pet.

Feel free to note yours down. Or if you're feeling brave, ask the people you work with.

Manage thyself

If you want to maximise productivity, it's worth optimising your weekly schedule to make the best use of the weekly energy highs and lows. For example, I'll prioritise Mondays and Tuesdays for design work, because these are the times when I'm at my most innovative. I also bias my meetings depending on how much effort I think they'll take. A new client is usually going to require a bit more mental effort and dedication from me, so I try to plan meetings with high-value prospects early in the week (but in the afternoon – remember, I uni-task in the mornings). This means they are getting well-rested, vibrant and bouncy Sarah.

It also means I can have my low-energy meetings on Fridays. When I say low-energy, I mean one of the following:

- **Low expectation** in terms of immediate revenue generation. For whatever reason, I've decided to take the pressure off myself to sell, sell, sell, now, now, *now*! Maybe I'm playing the long game with a prospect, or maybe it's one of those meetings to 'explore mutual synergies and potential collaboration opportunities'.[31]

- **Low effort** because being with this person is easy/fun/ invigorating, and so I feel like I've checked into a brain spa. I also use this time to take my most loyal clients for lunch somewhere that serves things like scallops in bergamot truffle beurre noisette and wild mushroom macarons paired with Assyrtiko wine from the black volcanoes of Santorini.[32] (I only mention it in case you're thinking of becoming a loyal client – I'll make it worth your while. Just saying.) In big handfuls: I throw myself into meaty work tasks at the start of the week and then I ease it back towards Friday.

But enough about me. What could your battle rhythm look like? I don't think you need to overthink this or be rigid about it. Of course, we all have to flex our schedules around new enquiries and work strands, peak periods and the occasional child falling out of a tree and requiring an unplanned trip to A&E. The point is, if you are aware of how your energy ebbs and flows during the day, week, and even from season to season, you can be a bit more intentional about optimising your work schedule.

Implementing uni-tasking into your busy day

By now, you should have a pretty good idea of how to establish your uni-tasks, so it's time to step up the Jedi training. We're going to incorporate these into the work cycle. I mentioned this previously when we looked at common barriers – you may recall the Aviate, Navigate, Communicate, Administrate work cycle we had in flying. The main benefit of a work cycle is that it allows us to be intentional about where we are focusing our attention even when the world has other ideas. It also proves that no matter how much you've got going on, *it's still possible to uni-task.*

Below is a visual representation of what a work cycle might look like. Note that in this visual, the uni-task is 'Fly the aircraft', and it goes in the centre of the work cycle.

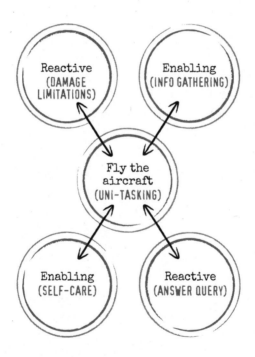

The Advanced Uni-tasking Work Cycle

Now, let's walk through it with your uni-task in mind. Let's say that your uni-task was designing a kick-ass presentation. That goes in the middle. Now, let's imagine all the things that might distract you from working on that presentation.

First, you might decide you need to get an image to put in your presentation. You'll notice in the diagram I've called that 'info gathering' and we will tell ourselves we have to switch our focus at this stage, because this is an enabling task. So, you might look back through your photos and, in doing so, notice that you were looking a little fitter in your holiday photos, and maybe you should renew that gym membership after all. Come to think of it, they were offering a discount code, which might be expiring soon. Suddenly this task seems like the most important task ever (I can relate – I am *really* vain).

Do you see how easy it is to derail your efforts to stay focused on your top priority? And remember, this is a task that is high importance and high impact. So here are a few questions to consider:

- Do you really need to switch focus? Ask yourself, 'Is this something I can kill in two minutes?' If it's more than two minutes, your brain will get embedded in the new task and when you go back to your 'Fly the aircraft' priority, it will feel like you're starting again. In this case, it's better to make a note of it and come back to it later.

- Could you put a placeholder in your presentation? 'Insert an adorable image that makes me look fabulous, humble and family-orientated and conveys the right amount of desirability without making it all about me.' (I'm sharing my scary inner monologue to demonstrate that 'quickly' diverting from the current task is often not as straightforward as we think.)

Rule of thumb: switch your focus only if it's critical to the central task right now and if you can kill it in two minutes.[33] Switch focus intentionally and verbally. If you decide that you really do need to carry out that enabling task right away, that's fine. After all, there's no point flying an aircraft in a beautifully straight line if you're heading directly into controlled airspace: there are times I needed to switch my focus from 'Fly the aircraft' to navigating, so I believe you if the same is true for you. For example, perhaps your task is time-sensitive, and you can't put off enabling tasks till later. If so, here's a ninja trick: *say it out loud.* 'I'm going to get an image of X, and then I'll come back to the presentation.'

The brain is brilliant at making the things we say come true. The unconscious brain fulfils the commands of our conscious brain, which is why positive affirmations work and why fortune tellers steal a living.[34] So, say it out loud to remind yourself why you're switching focus, and then you've got half a chance of staying focused on the job. If you want a gorgeous example of this (and I mean gorgeous), just watch the opening scene of *Top Gun: Maverick* (yes, I am talking about that film again) when he takes Dark Star for her Mach 10 test flight and listen to his 'patter' (eg, 'Needles live, temperatures rising, engines responding, we're looking good...'). The point is that we verbalise what we are doing all the time, usually so the rest of the crew knows what is going on. But even single-seat pilots like Tom Cruise keep this patter up, and I realised the unintended consequence of this was that it allows us to be intentional about where we focus our attention. If you say what you are focusing on, then funnily enough, you'll focus on it.

If you want proof of this, remember the last time you were only half listening to a conversation with another person? Have you ever come out with some complete non-sequitur unrelated to the conversation, but strangely aligned to what you were thinking at the time?

'Darling, what shall we have for dinner?'

'Hmm, yes, I will have a look in the gym and see what offers there are.'

The same is true for reactive tasks. Let's say you have a particular person you will always answer the phone to no matter how deeply you are in flow or how important your work task is (for me, it's the school, or maybe Tom Cruise). You can apply the same methodology. Intentionally switch your focus, say it out loud, and then bring your attention back to your 'Fly the aircraft' priority once you've completed this reactive task.

I've added another version of an enabling task to the work cycle, which I've called self-care. I'm not saying you *have* to switch your focus to this – at this point, I'm merely referring to the fact that you might need to break your flow to go the loo. Equally, if you think a walk around the block or a bit of fresh air would help while you're doing deep work, then go ahead. You know yourself best.

The point is this: if you decide you really do have to switch focus in the middle of your high-impact, high-important task, do it intentionally and verbalise your focus. Remember, it's always better to take control of where your attention is than to be hostage to whatever thought or image popped up last.

Minimise the penalty of uni-tasking

Once you have finished your uni-task, or you've come to a natural break in concentration, then you can do what I like to refer to as your damage limitation tasks. This is where you will sweep up reactive tasks that you've postponed during your uni-tasking. (You may recall I previously referred to this decision to postpone as, 'Let's talk about it on the ground.') It might be replying to a WhatsApp. It might be coming back to a colleague who has asked for help (more on that later). As I mentioned before, this is usually the point I'll check my emails just in case there is a time-sensitive email I need to respond to.

When I advocate uni-tasking, I'm not suggesting you focus on one thing for your entire day. I understand you have other priorities, and not all tasks have to be uni-tasks. So, be deliberate about which tasks you uni-task. I also understand that when you are uni-tasking, there may still be some reasons for you to switch your focus. The work cycle gives you a way to be intentional about *how* you switch that focus. The big win from using a work cycle is that it creates a mindset that allows you to be in charge of where you focus your attention. Once you've identified your uni-task, you can use the work cycle to help you stay on track despite distractions.

✂ Why the juice is worth the squeeze

Imagine you go into hospital for a routine operation. You're supposed to be having your appendix removed, but the surgeon looks distracted and asks vaguely if you are here for sterilisation. While the surgeon is preparing you for surgery, they ask you a series of questions, but you notice whenever you respond they look glazed. At one point, they try (and fail) to discreetly check their phone. Just before you are about to be given a general anaesthetic, you hear the surgeon utter, 'Bollocks, I forgot to renew my car tax. You guys make a start and I'll join you shortly.' This might sound far-fetched to the point of ridicule, but what if you were to go back and change some of the keywords for non-medical terms? You might just be describing yourself on a very distracted day.

The point is that you wouldn't settle for it – and neither will your customers. If you want to produce first-class service, truly understand your customers' needs and earn unbeatable trust in your products, you need to give your full attention to *one* thing at a time. If you don't, your customers will know, and they'll vote with their feet.

No matter how tempting it is to cut corners or try to cram 'one more thing' in, it just doesn't pay to give half of your attention to your high-value tasks. In the end, uni-tasking will win you more business and earn you more loyalty.

Your customers aren't automatically top priority

This brings me on to my next point. Do not confuse the power of undivided attention with being completely hostage to every whim of your customer. Having gone to the trouble of working out which tasks will have the most meaningful impact towards your desired outcomes, it would be a travesty to ignore them and focus on whatever (or whoever) has just popped up in your workflow. This is why you need to have a strategy for dealing with your customers, because while the objective is to provide them with excellent service, there is more than one way to do that.

Ultimately, you serve your customer best if you are giving the very best of yourself, and it might serve you (and your customer) better to focus on whatever you are doing at that moment: training your team, business development, collecting your child from school, or whatever. The customer is not always your top priority. Let me share a story which illustrates this.

CASE STUDY: Letting someone down

We were in Kenya supporting the Army when we heard that a soldier had been bitten by a black mamba snake. Do you know how long you've got left to live when you've been bitten by a black mamba snake? Not long is the answer. In military CASEVAC, everything is the 'golden hour', so we were working on the assumption we had sixty minutes to get the medic to our soldier before he was dead.

It was the darkest night I had ever seen. Even wearing my night vision goggles, I couldn't see anything. I was gripped with fear. But we were this soldier's only hope.

Usually, at night, we wouldn't transit any lower than about 150 m above the ground. But as soon as we weighed up the conditions, we realised we couldn't transit at that height or we would be in the cloud, so we made the decision to transit below the normal operating height. I was breaking a legal order. We were taking a big risk. And it was really bloody dark. I remember feeling seriously out of my depth, but my crew seemed to have faith in my flying ability and my decisions, so we forged on.

When we reached the vicinity of the casualty, we dropped even lower. The granularity still wasn't good enough for me to see the ground. I remember saying, 'I feel like I'm going to run out of ability here.' Inside, my heart was in my mouth, but I said it in a measured and slow way. I expected my crew to agree with me, but instead, my crewman said, 'What about if I hang out of the side door and shine a light? You could fly down the beam?' So, I canted the tail of my helicopter towards the hillside and we crabbed our way along with just enough light for me to make out the texture of the hillside. At this point, we were 10 m above the ground.

We got to within 0.1 miles of our casualty. Then two things happened: the view out of the front started to go grey and misty (we were on the brink of going into cloud) and the low-height alarm went off, which meant we were seconds from impacting the ground.

It was obvious the mission was doomed. I badly wanted to fly home, but it's a hard decision to leave a man to die. So, we went round again. And again. And again.

Every time, the same thing happened. I was sandwiched between the ground and the cloud, with nowhere to go. Eventually, I announced to my crew, 'I'm sorry, I think we need to turn back.' We returned in silence. I felt like a complete failure.

When we landed, we debriefed the mission, and it was at this point my crew said, 'We would have backed whatever decision you made, but we were fucking relieved when you finally said you were turning back.' I was shocked. I felt like I'd been the first one to bottle it. It was only then that I noticed every single one of us was shaking.

'But you all seemed so calm!' I said.

'The only reason we were calm is because *you* were calm!' And it dawned on me. We were all scared we were going to die, but there was something even more terrifying than death. Letting someone else down.

The point is: I understand how strongly we desire to serve our customers and that it will feel almost impossible to say no to them. But you cannot serve your customers if you are a smoking hole in the ground. And if you run a team, remember that they trust you more than you probably realise. Know this: they will follow you into that smoking hole. That's a hell of a responsibility. How do you reconcile that? Well, here's a tip. Don't think about who you are saying no to. I wasn't saying no to the man on the hill. I was saying *yes* to me and my crew so we could live to fight another day.

We are hard-wired to be people-pleasers, and we want to say yes. So, work with the brain instead of against it. Try this: *the intentional yes*. Be intentional about what you say yes to, who you say yes to, and when you say yes to it. And make it a 100% 'Hell, yes!' Give it your full attention. Because remember, that's how we ultimately do *our* best work and serve our customers the best.

Oh, and the soldier? He was fine. Turns out his snake recognition was woeful. He wasn't bitten by a black mamba. In fact, he wasn't even bitten by a snake. He was bitten by a spider. So, he lived. And so will your customers.

Key takeaways

- This entire system has *one* purpose. To get you started. While it may feel daunting to prioritise, the truth is you're capable of it. The trick is just to get going. The more you practise, the easier you'll find it, and the more you do it, the more you can refine your processes.

- Think of it like being on a firing range. Every time we did pistol or rifle shooting, we would first fire five rounds on the target. Then, we'd have a look at where they landed. Most of the time, the rounds would not have fallen on the bullseye, so we'd adjust. Then we'd fire a few more rounds. And then have another look at the target. And make more adjustments. And bit by bit, we'd bring our rounds onto target. You can apply exactly the same principle to uni-tasking. I just want you to be the *best* version of you, and you'll do that by giving your full attention to one thing at time. The key to all of this is to put down those first five sighting rounds.

- Not all tasks are created equal. Prioritising is hard, but it's not impossible, and it gets easier the more you practise it. The trick is to get started and then adjust as you go.

- Schedule an hour with the aim of completing twenty minutes of uni-tasking. If you get distracted, use your hook to come back uni-tasking.

- Our energy drains throughout the day and the week. Scheduling your uni-tasking to coincide with the high-energy times of your days and weeks will optimise your performance. Similarly, you can schedule easier/less important tasks or energy-boosting tasks for those daily and weekly lows.

Commitment to action

Complete the two matrices to identify your high-impact, high-energy tasks. These are your uni-tasks. Identify the times of day and week you will be most able to give your full attention and your A game to uni-tasking (this may need to be a compromise between your high-energy time of day and your likelihood of being distracted by others). And you're off!

6

I Is For Interferences

BOTTOM LINE UP FRONT

Uncomfortable truth:

The world will survive without you. Sorry, but it's true.

Business gains:

Longer periods of deep work to achieve higher-quality service or product. Greater self-sufficiency of your teams, paving the way for growth and succession. Build stronger customer relationships.

Personal gains:

Free up time to do the things that you love with the people you love.

You can only be in one place at any one time

Let's try a little exercise. You can do this at work, or with family/friends. I do this exercise in workshops, but also around the family dinner table and it's great fun.

EXERCISE: Three-way conversation

Get into a group of three. Number yourselves 'Person 1, 2, 3', etc.

- Person 1 starts a conversation with a simple sentence about their plan for the weekend. For example: 'This weekend, I'm going to the movies.'

- Person 2 then follows with their plans for the weekend: 'I'm going swimming with my kids.'

- Person 3 then needs to start with the last word that Person 1 said (in this case, movies): 'Movies are good, but I would rather be in the pub.'

- Now, back to Person 1, who needs to start with the last word from Person 2 (in this case, kids): 'Kids are great when they are quiet.'

- Person 2 then starts with the last word from Person 3. (In this case, it was pub): 'Pub quizzes are good.'

The three-way conversation

By the time you've gone around the circle once, everyone has to start with the last word of the person who went last but one. After five to ten minutes, you can stop the exercise.

During the exercise, you'll probably notice a few things:

- You were focused exclusively on what the last person but one said.

- You remember nothing of what the person in between you said.

- The conversation was unnatural, didn't flow and, at times, was utterly ludicrous.

Now imagine the people in the exercise are your customers. In other words, imagine you're trying to have multiple conversations at once. Communication lines are crisscrossing in the ether like a game of drunk adult Twister, but with less laughing and far worse consequences. The point is this: you cannot be in two places at once. If you're trying to have conversations with more than one client at a time, it will show. At best, you'll be giving a half-arsed service to one of them, or your communication will be unclear and clunky. Don't do it.

A strategy for different types of clients

What you need is a strategy for dealing with different types of clients that allows you to give them the attention they deserve (not that they demand). So, let's get straight into it. I've got another matrix for you.

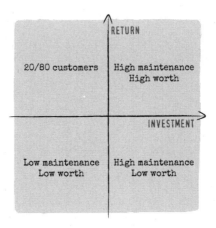

The Return-on-Investment Matrix

High-return low-investment

Let's start with these customers, because they are your holy grail. A high-ROI customer is someone who gives *a lot* back in comparison to what you put in. I don't mean you ignore them (in fact, it's the opposite). Typically, these customers pay well and on time, give you repeat business and/or refer you to other clients. The return on your investment (in them) is very *high*. Return is often measured in terms of direct revenue, but it could also be in terms of reputation, exposure, credibility or onward referrals. Tim Ferriss talks about this as the Pareto Principle or 20/80 rule (ie, 20% of our customers provide 80% of our revenue).[35]

If you want to run your business efficiently, then it's a good idea to identify and prioritise these customers. It may seem obvious, but it's quite easy to take these customers for granted because they are comparatively low maintenance. Often, in business and in life, it's the squeaky wheel that gets the grease. We might focus our efforts on customers in the top-right of the matrix instead, but if we want to make the best use of our time and attention, my advice is to make sure these high-return low-investment customers feel special and loved because they are your highest-performing customers. It's a good idea to make sure you know who they are (I use my XERO software to identify my top ten customers each year) and then work out how to keep them. Of course, strategies for maintaining these high-value relationships will vary, but here are some of my favourite ideas:

- **Tell them they are special.** I remember doing an online course with a speaker coach. She started the session by saying, 'Sarah is one of my star customers because she gives me repeat business, and she refers people to me.' I positively levitated off the seat (don't judge, we *all* like being a teacher's pet from time to time), and I made damn sure I stayed on that pedestal. Don't be afraid of telling people upfront that they are your top customers. People need to hear that stuff from time to time.

- **Mark key occasions.** Put them on your Christmas card list. Maybe even celebrate anniversaries with them – 'It's been five years since we met!'

- **Invite them to special days out.** These could be Wimbledon, Henley Regatta, Goodwood Festival of Speed (I'm just mentioning my favourite days out here, in case anyone reading this book feels like giving me special treatment).

- **Build goodwill for referrals by referring business to them.** It's so easy to think, 'How can I get more business from my top-performing clients?' But the best way to build relationships is to think, 'How can I get more business *for* my top-performing clients?' For example, if you know someone who is looking for a recruitment specialist and one of your best clients has expertise in this area, make the introduction for them. Anytime they refer business to you, send them a thank you gift.

- **Get to know them so you can serve them better.** Take them for lunch. Ask how they're doing and how you can support them. (You might get more business out of it, and even if you don't, you can think of it as market research while nurturing your best relationships.)

- **Clone them.** Ask yourself, 'Why are they such good customers?' Do they come from a certain industry? Are they in a certain geographic area? Demographic? Are they the perfect match for your product or services? Are they a similar mindset to you? If so, you've just identified your customer avatar. Find other prospects who are like them and get ready to build your portfolio of high-performing customers.

- **Learn from them.** Think back to when they were a new client. How did you identify them in the first place? How did you find them, or how did you attract them? Unless you are very lucky, there was probably a bit more investment upfront to get them to become high-performing customers. So, ask yourself, 'What did I do right with this customer? What was the psychological contracting and the type of communication? What were the expectations?' Be curious about the process that you used. It may have felt intuitive if the customer was a great match, but be prepared to pick apart what you did and how you did it, and you've got a great roadmap to turn all of your customers into high-performing ones.

Which brings me to the top-right corner.

High-return high-investment

These are customers who give high returns, but also require high investment in terms of time, money or energy. You could think of these customers has high maintenance, but also high worth. (Think of your favourite celeb – they're probably high maintenance, but who doesn't want them as a customer?) If you've got a few customers like that, it's not difficult to see how you might end up playing communication Twister all over again trying to keep these people happy.

Typically, new customers or prospects will also need higher investment because you have to work harder at the beginning to earn their trust. So, my advice is to have a defined strategy for dealing with these customers skilfully that manages your time and energy effectively. It's also useful to consider how you can get them to move from the top-right to the top-left. The following strategies are designed with energy and attention management in mind. I'm not telling you how to run your business; I'm offering some ideas on how you can build your relationships so that they are both stronger and easier to manage.

Meet them where they're at

First things first. Meet them where they're at. Imagine that you're attending a networking session. This session includes an ice-breaker session where you are asked to identify yourself as either an introvert or an extrovert by standing on one side of the room or another. Now, I know I mentioned earlier that I'm an extrovert because I get energy from speaking to others, but I get energy from speaking to others on a *one-to-one basis*. So, when I walk into a room of people I don't know, I want to talk quietly to someone in the corner and then another person in another corner until I've got to know a few people and overcome my shyness.

Here's the thing. I don't want to draw attention to my shyness by being asked to stand on the 'introvert' side of the room for everyone to see. Surprised, aren't you? The point is that putting people in boxes or labelling them is risky. At best, it's lazy. At worst, we risk making them feel uncomfortable. Imagine that you put yourself in the introvert camp and then someone shouts across the room, 'No way! You're definitely an extrovert,' and all eyes turn to you. I would want the ground to swallow me up at this stage. Furthermore, I'd become disengaged and distrustful. This is the last thing we want our customers to be, right?

The lesson is this: don't try and force your customers to be something they are not just to make your life easier. It's a fast way to ruin the relationship. Meet them where they are at first, and then you can work out how to meet in the middle. The first thing you need to do is talk to them and understand how they like to work. Just ask them.

Turn yourself into a high-return low-investment seller

If you can put your customers into high-maintenance and low-maintenance boxes, the same is true for you as a seller.

We all know those times when we've got fed up trying to buy a product because the process was too clunky. We had to sign up for an account that we didn't want. Their website makes you enter your details every single time you try and buy something. They make it impossible to unsubscribe. You have to wait for hours on the phone line listening to 'The girl from Ipanema' on repeat. You have to hunt down your delivery because it ended up at the pizza shop next door, and you threw the 'we missed you' note in the bin.

The point is this: you do not want the customer to have to work hard to give you their business. You want to be nice and low maintenance for them. (Please don't confuse this with being desperate – 'easy to work with' doesn't mean dropping everything for them.) A good idea is to ask them, 'What can I do to make your life easier?'

I did this recently with a customer who was teetering on being in the top-right corner. They would sometimes give little nudges in the runup to deadlines. I wanted to go in and read them the riot act, wag my finger and tell them that every time they distracted me, it would delay the delivery of my product, but I figured that would be a bit of a dick move and unlikely to work. So instead, I said to myself, 'If I can just understand why they are like that, it might help me to be a bit more understanding and will piss me off less, which will distract me less.' In the course of the conversation, I learned a few things I could do proactively to stop them from chasing me in the runup to a deadline, and they identified for themselves that they didn't need to chase me. And right there, we'd stumbled on the critical ingredient that customers need to be low-maintenance. *Trust.* What's more, we realised we already had a high level of trust in each other. They didn't chase me again after that call. And I was able to do a few things proactively to reinforce that trust.

Hopefully, you get the idea: a lot of the work in getting the customer to be less needy is actually understanding what they need to decide to trust you. Once you've gained their trust, you can tell them how *you* like to work.

Train the customer (on how you like to work)

For example: 'OK, I know this is the first time we've worked together, so it might be useful to explain how I deliver my best work for you…' In my case, I might say: 'This is the date I'll submit the work. Instead of bothering you with updates and disrupting your work, I'll guarantee the work will be in your inbox at our agreed deadline. Of course, if you want to check anything or provide any further info, you can drop me an email but otherwise you won't hear from me. Does that work for you?'

They might say, 'Great! Once we've agreed this work, I don't really want to think about it again until it's in front of me.' Or they might say, 'Actually, I do like to be kept in the loop, so I know it's progressing OK.' In which case, I might respond, 'OK, how about if I send a couple of updates, with three days to go and on the morning…'

I think you get the idea. I'm a solopreneur and a speaker, and this works for me. Take what you need from it. The point is that everyone works a little differently and might be a bit high-maintenance to start with, but building trust is a great way to move customers from the top-right to the top-left. Then you can hopefully enjoy strong but easy-going relationships with your top clients. That's a great way to maximise your time and energy.

Low-return customers

I'm not going to cover these customers in detail, because I've prioritised the high-return customers (ie, the ones that are above the line). All I'll say is this: if a customer is a low-return high-investment (ie, takes more from you than they give back), well, do you really need them? Could you put them in the 'discard' box?

Also think about the signal you send to your peers or colleagues if you are prepared to turn away business from people who are a pain in the arse to work with. You're saying, 'My (team) morale and welfare means more to me than making an extra bit of cash.' What you get back in terms of team/peer loyalty is something that is hard to beat. This brings me neatly to my next point. While we've talked about getting the most out of our customers, there are others we interact with, too – our colleagues.

'Bubble buts'

I touched on this in an earlier chapter and I'm sure you have all come across them. Now let's examine how we deal with this challenge.

The 'bubble but' is someone who knowingly bursts your 'mission bubble'. They have the awareness to know you are highly engaged in your current task, but they've decided to interrupt you anyway. You know they know this because they acknowledge it in their first greeting. (For solopreneurs, read 'colleagues' as friends/family. Basically, anyone who's likely to interrupt you – like my partner! Wait – he won't be interrupting *you*. Oh, you know what I mean!)

In your workplace, it might sound like this:

- Have you got a minute?

- I know you're busy but…

- Is this a bad time?

- I just need a quick five minutes of your time. (It's never quick, and it's never five minutes.)

Now, don't be too quick to judge. We've *all* been that person, because when we are stressed, we prioritise everything as urgent and important. So, bubble buts will genuinely believe that whatever they've got going on is more urgent and more important than anything you've got going on.

CASE STUDY: Mission interrupted

Picture the scene. We are in Afghanistan. We've just been tasked with a mission of national strategic importance: providing high-level cover to convoys on a major supply route through known areas of hostile forces. It's imperative this convoy reaches its destination: the lorries in that convoy carry the much-needed resupply of ballistic body armour, combat tourniquets and the new limited-edition Ben and Jerry's ice cream to our airbase. Naturally, we've planned the mission meticulously. We've factored in every contingency we can think of.

We've loaded the helicopters with ammunition and water. We're kitted up like Rambo: combat tourniquet in the left arm pocket, first field dressing in left leg pocket, eight magazines of 7.62 mm. We've sanitised our kit so that if we get captured, we can't be exploited. We are about to walk out into the hot, dark, dusty night. We can hear the gentle hum of a Hercules gunship in the distance, getting ready to give us overwatch. We are revved up and ready to go, feeling slightly scared, but also feeling a sense of connectedness that we are all scared together.

And then someone appears in the periphery. They have a solemn look on their face. A mission update? An increase in threat to friendly forces?

They whisper these words... 'I know you're in your bubble... But...' And then they ask you a question about the upcoming quiz night.

The bottom line is that it's as irritating as hell when someone projects their urgent important priorities onto you – *especially* if they are not urgent important to you. Expecting people to prioritise their tasks in the same way that you would prioritise them isn't realistic. In fact, it's not even desirable. If you think about how to maximise output as a team, everyone needs to have different priorities so that they don't all focus on the same task, duplicate work and get under each other's feet. In other words, people *need* to have different priorities so they can work simultaneously on complementary work strands. I'm not saying people should work in silos (I know there is lots of hoo-ha these days about working collaboratively), but let's not confuse working together with stealing each other's sandwiches.

While we're talking about collaboration, we also need people who have different strengths and think differently from us so we can work on alternative and complementary work strands to multiply our output. What we need, then, is a strategy for respecting everybody's priorities and ways of working while also protecting our own bubble.

Training colleagues to be more self-sufficient (less needy)

To get the best performance from a team, we need to empower cognitively diverse people to work on the things that they are good at with a degree of self-sufficiency.

Let's look at this from the beginning. It's not unreasonable to expect new colleagues to be a bit more needy. There will be things they need to learn: the idiosyncrasies of a particular role, or perhaps learning and inculcating company values. In short, they need to learn new behaviours. Keep in mind that learning doesn't happen in a neat, straight line, either. Studies of behaviour change show that the path to greatness is actually rather higgledy-piggledy, with plenty of setbacks. In fact, if there aren't any setbacks, then it's not a change in behaviour; it's the same behaviour with a different name. Inevitably experiencing lapses is actually a positive sign, because it means that we are genuinely committed to learning a new behaviour.

Once the initial, upfront training has started to bed in though, we need to inspire our work colleagues to become more self-sufficient and continue learning for themselves rather than leaning on others all the time. In many ways, it's not dissimilar to training the customer. First, meet them where they are. If they've interrupted you in the flap, it's obviously something they care about. It's a good idea to acknowledge that. Here are some examples of validating responses:

- 'I can see this is important.' (Acknowledge their priorities.)

- 'I'd like to give this the attention it deserves.' (Demonstrate their value.)

- 'I have some time between X and Y. When would work for you?' (Respect your own time.)

Clearly, you can adapt the above as you see fit, but the principles are as follows.

Acknowledge their priorities (meet them where they are at)

Demonstrate that you take their issue seriously. You will see from the example that there is also some signalling going on here – the implied message is, 'I'll give you a better service if I can give this my undivided attention later rather than my divided attention right now.' You are gently educating them that uni-tasking is a better form of service than multi-tasking. You're gently telling them how *you* like to work. And who knows, they might be inspired to follow your example.

Protect your own boundaries while establishing a compromise

The example response may be overly elaborate for you. There may be some people who would see right through this or find it patronising. Everyone is different. That's half the fun of this. Its purpose is to give you the space to think about the people you interact with and which strategies will work best for you *and* them.

Of course, by the time you've said all of this, your bubble has already burst. (Don't forget: you can resume your focus by using techniques from Habit A). The objective, in this case, is to play the long game. By signalling how you like to work, you're effectively training your colleague. Stick with it. You will see that the interruptions will reduce over time when they realise that being a bubble but doesn't win them an immediate answer.

If this all sounds a bit hard-nosed, take heart. It's not just you who benefits from this approach. Remember, one of the biggest barriers to uni-tasking is a lack of confidence in our ability to prioritise. Well, that's often what happens to other people. Except it's not a lack of confidence to prioritise. It's a lack of confidence, full stop. Often, people come to us for help because they don't trust themselves to find their own solutions. In this case, we need to give them the space to find confidence in their own answers. Here are two things you can try when someone asks for help:

1. **Face to face:** Ask them, 'What do you think?' Often, people want validation that they've arrived at the 'right' conclusion, but when you give validation, they continue looking for it. And who's to say your answer is the right answer anyway? We've hired these people to use their brains; we might as well get them to use them. So, rather than giving them approval, ask them the above question so they can give themselves the approval they need.

2. **Email or text:** Apply the twenty-minute rule (ie, leave it twenty minutes before you reply). In my experience, most people have figured out the answer

for themselves by then, particularly if it is urgent and important. Or they've figured out it's not as urgent as they thought, which means you've helped them to reprioritise. Either way, a little bit of ghosting can actually be doing them a favour. Boom!

Another strategy I've learned is asking people to put it into an email. If people say to you (in person or on the phone) that, 'It's easier to talk it through with you,' it's often because they haven't really thought the problem through. They don't really understand the root problem they are trying to solve, and they haven't used their available resources to find their own solution. So, the conversation is really them verbalising their thoughts and workshopping all this stuff out. That's fine if it's a coaching call and you're being paid for your time. But if you're running a business, you're taking time out from doing your job to help them work out how to do their job. Sometimes it will be necessary to do this (eg, with the newbies), but a lot of the time being gentle but firm is a better option.

The reason you'll resist this

I remember someone saying to me, 'Your superpower, Sarah, is that you *are just enough* of a bitch.' I laughed insouciantly, but inside, I was crushed. The last thing in the world I want is for people to dislike me, and the last time I checked, being described as a bitch is not a great testament to one's likeability.

This is why it is so hard to protect our boundaries (or our bubbles): we are terrified that if we do, we'll be seen as hard-nosed, uncompromising and selfish. Here's the truth: some people will decide to interpret it that way. The methods I've outlined above will hopefully reduce the likelihood of this happening, but people are people. We get upset for all sorts of daft reasons that we often don't really understand, so there might be times when people decide to take it personally if you don't drop everything for them. Of course, that will be upsetting.

But here is another truth: you will survive, and in all likelihood, so will your relationship. We tend to assume that any conflict or tension in a relationship is a shattering failure, but that's a very unrealistic expectation. Even if you attempt to avoid all confrontation by going along with everything others say, at some point, other people's priorities will conflict, so you'll wind up pissing someone off eventually. The fact is this – there is no earthly way to please everyone all the time.

It's also time to let yourself off the hook when it comes to believing that you have to be a 'people-pleaser' in order to be a good person. We are hard-wired to people-please for the simple fact that we want to be liked. Or because we don't want to deal with the discomfort of acknowledging our actions have upset others. In other words, 'people-pleasing' is ultimately a self-serving coping strategy to protect us from the sting of rejection or shame. Having the courage to let people think what they like about you says more about you and your respect for them than needing them to like you does. In short, be just enough of a bitch. (The person who made that comment is now my fiancé, so take that as proof that your relationships can survive!)

Final note: *don't be a bubble but.* Of course, this should go without saying, but if you don't want people to burst your bubble, then don't burst theirs. Before you throw your hands in the air and demand to be rescued, ask yourself, 'Is this genuinely urgent, or have I confused importance with urgency? What's the impact on them if I ask them this right now? What is the problem here and can I solve this problem in another way?' You might just surprise yourself at how bloody awesome you are.

CASE STUDY: Do the job

I was privileged enough to fly Special Forces (SF) missions during my time in the RAF. Being selected to fly these missions was something I drew immense pride from. The missions were of the utmost strategic importance to our national security. We really were making the world safer (or so we hoped), and we had to get it right. Great care was taken over which pilots were selected. Only the best were picked, so in this sense, it did feel very special to be a Special Forces pilot. And I'd made the cut. Except for one small problem.

I'm a woman. No female helicopter pilots had flown SF missions before, so nobody really knew what the form was. A senior pilot dismissed it out of hand: 'There is no way you can fly SF missions, Sarah. For one, the camps they operate out of are men only. There are no facilities for women.' I looked at him uncomprehendingly. 'There are no female showers!' He spelled out. 'You'd have to share a communal shower block with no privacy.' An image of chiselled, bronzed, handsome men flashed into my head. I had to suppress an urge to whoop loudly.

'I'll be fine with that,' I reassured him. Feeling the need to feign modesty, I declared that I would shower in a swimming costume. In the end, they were communal, but they had cubicles, so there really had been no need to worry. That said, unaccustomed to female company, I did, more than once, exit my cubicle to encounter a chiselled, bronzed, handsome man towelling himself down. They were never fazed by this. They'd just say, 'Good morning,' cheerfully and go about their day. I'll give the SF boys this – they are utterly professional. (I, on the other hand, would walk around with a grin like a Cheshire Cat for the rest of the day, and my fellow pilots would eye-roll me repeatedly.) Anyway, we agreed I didn't have a problem with the accommodation arrangements.

But there was another issue. I'd compromise the mission. If we got shot down in the middle of hostile territory, the SF boys would feel obliged to protect me, which means they'd compromise their own mission to save my skin. They had planned these missions for months, including the exact moment to execute their mission. They had a tiny window of opportunity and needed to execute their mission with deadly precision. And these highly strategic missions would be compromised all because of me.

Apparently, there was no way around this. 'They wouldn't be able to help themselves; they'd *have* to protect you because, you know, you're a *woman*.' I suspected they were underestimating, not just me, but the professionalism of the SF. So, I called their bullshit. I asked, 'Could we ask the SF what would happen if the helicopter went down?' The answer that came back was this. 'If we go down in the middle of the mission, you won't see us. We'll disappear into the night. And we'll be running – faster than any of you can run – toward our target.'

I remember when the other pilots learned this, they were forced to confront an uncomfortable truth. We were there to do a job, and the SF boys expected us to do our job. They expected us to get them from A to B safely, and they expected us to be able to look after ourselves and step up to the mark so that they could get on with doing their job. They weren't there to be our personal bodyguards.

It was quite amusing to see how this news rattled them. I felt pretty scared, too. I'm a pilot, not a soldier, after all. But I also remember feeling proud that these incredibly capable people trusted that I could step up to the mark, even though it would have been uncomfortable. I knew that by stepping up to the mark, I was enabling something so much bigger than I could have dreamed of achieving on my own, so I thought to myself, 'Hell yeah, I can do this!'

I hope you can see the parallels. To get the best from our team, we need to do what *we* are good at while allowing those in our team to get on with what *they* are good at. That will require people to have a degree of self-sufficiency. And that will inevitably require people to get used to feeling a bit uncomfortable. And guess what? We are far more capable of that than we realise.

I've already shared some of the ways we can nudge people to discover their true awesomeness – simply by resisting the temptation to immediately rescue them. But we can take that another step. We can train our colleagues proactively.

The art of skilful delegation

Remember the Urgent–Important Matrix from Habit B? We wrote down our weekly tasks and categorised them using this matrix. I suggested delegating urgent non-important tasks. Just to be clear, I'm not talking about fobbing off tasks you don't like to people you don't like. I think of it in these terms: it's not important that I do it, but it could be important that someone else does it. And herein lies the opportunity to delegate skilfully in a way that proactively develops others, which comes down to delegating outside our comfort zone.

The reason for this is twofold. First, we do our best work in our discomfort zone. You may recall from Habit H that when we are stressed, we produce lots of cortisol. Cortisol's chief job is to increase our alertness: it's what's responsible for waking us up in the morning; it's also what gives us precision focus when we are under pressure. So, cortisol in itself isn't bad. In fact, 'just the right amount' is what we need to perform at our best. We don't want to be totally freaking out. We don't want to be bored or fast asleep, either. We want to be just uncomfortable enough.

Second, discomfort builds resilience and self-trust. Every time we sit with a little bit of discomfort, we are providing our brains with evidence that we can survive discomfort. We are teaching our brains, 'Oh, I can do things that are uncomfortable, and I can survive them!' Because the brain is always growing neural pathways, it starts to rewire itself over time and we end up with a new core belief along the lines of, 'I can survive difficulty,' or, 'I can get through this,' or even, 'I'll be OK.' In other words, we train ourselves to feel more resilient and to build self-trust.

Tell me that's not something worth getting excited about. We'll talk more about how to develop this ability to sit with discomfort in Habit T, but for now, please trust me; it's a *good* thing to be able to operate out of our comfort zone.

How to delegate well

There are two keys to skilful delegation:

1. **Delegate slightly beyond the other person's comfort zone.** When you delegate a task, give them

just slightly more autonomy than they are comfortable with. They might resist this a bit – sometimes, people find autonomy quite scary because it also brings accountability. They might want you to hold their hand all the way so they don't have to think for themselves, but keep the faith; they will grow as a result.

2. **Delegate slightly beyond your comfort zone.** Give slightly more autonomy than you feel comfortable with. An easy way to do this is to replace instructions with information. When you assign a task, rather than micromanaging them to death and demanding they do it exactly how *you* would, just tell them the outcome you're looking for and let them decide how they'll do it.

Many high achievers find it hard to relinquish control. We tell ourselves we are neglecting our duty to others, but by doing this (relinquishing control), we are demonstrating that we trust them and that we're prepared to put our money where our mouth is. Besides, they might just come up with some brilliant way of doing it that we'd have never thought of. Remember, there is no point in having brilliant, cognitively diverse people on your team if they are not empowered to think for themselves.

Yes day

If you'd like to prove to yourself that it's possible to relinquish a bit of control without the world ending, here is something you can try: the 'yes day'. I nicked the idea from the film with the same title, where the parents have a yes day with their kids.

The idea is to teach the parents to trust their children more and loosen their iron grip.

The principle is simple. For an entire day, whoever you are responsible for can ask to do whatever they want, and you have to say yes. You can put some basic safety and financial boundaries in place if you like, but hopefully, you get the idea.

I tried it with my child so I could prove the concept (I've always maintained I've learned my best leadership lessons through parenting). I remember the day arrived and he shrieked with delight.

'I've already got my first question!' he said. I prepared myself for the worst. 'Can I go for a poo… In the bushes?' I shrugged and said yes. This was going to be easier than I thought. Next, we pulled up outside a newsagent. 'Can I buy all the sweeties in the shop?' he asked. I said yes, but I decided to give him some information, too: the RDA of sugar for an eight-year-old is 28 mg. Which is roughly equivalent to a bag of Maltesers. Regular exceedance of the RDA has been proven to cause diabetes. Which can cause blindness and amputation of limbs. He came back with an apple.

I hadn't said no or given him instructions, but I had given him information, and he'd made a good choice. The point is this: when we give people more autonomy and trust, not only do they thrive, but they'll also pleasantly surprise you. They might even surpass your wildest expectations in terms of their competence and capability.

You might resist this, too, thinking:

- I can't trust others to do the job as well as me.

- I'm the only person that can do what I do.

- If you want something done properly, you need to do it yourself.

- My team need me to make the decisions.

- My team can't do it without me.

- If I'm not there to sort it out, the world will end.

Do you know what these statements all have in common? They are all lies. I'm sorry to say this, but you are not indispensable. Nor should you be. We covered this when we looked at common barriers, but I'll reiterate it here. You deserve to take some holiday once in a while. At some point, you will also have earned the right to retire to that big yacht you've been dreaming of, which will only be possible if you can hand over your beloved job to someone else. So please, however this limiting belief manifests itself, just let it go. At some point, we need to let others do our job as well as we can. Maybe even a little better than we can.

Why the juice is worth the squeeze

When I was promoted to Squadron Leader, I was no longer 'just a pilot'. I had to do some leadership stuff, too. So, I did a lot less flying than previously. I still reckoned I was one of the best pilots on the squadron, though. In fact, I prided myself on being better, stronger, faster, cleverer and funnier than everyone in my team. Because that's what a good leader is, right? They are better than everyone else, and everyone knows it… Luckily, a good friend, who had also just been promoted, gave me a kick up the arse early on. He said, 'What if some of the guys are now technically better at flying than you? Would that be a problem?' I realised it was only a problem for my ego. While I still had the duty of flying, my priority now was to make sure that my pilots were the best they could be – perhaps even better than me.

So, take it from me: the people around you are brilliant, just like you. And with your nurturing, they could be even better. When that happens, it's not a sign of weakness. It's a sign of terrific leadership and personal enlightenment.

Key takeaways

- Not all customers are created equal. Identifying your high return on investment customers is the first step to making the most of your time and attention.

- It is possible to 'train the customer' to be less high maintenance. We can start by finding out how they like to work and then finding a compromise with how you like to work.

- It's highly likely that your priorities will not be the same as other people's priorities. In fact, when you're working in a high-performing team, it's highly desirable, so we can collaborate and not duplicate. For this to work, people need to do what they are good at, to the best of their ability and with a degree of self-sufficiency.

- 'Bubble buts' are not bad people; they usually lack confidence in their own judgement. We can nudge them towards greater productivity and confidence by resisting the urge to rescue them immediately.

- Treat others as you like to be treated. Don't be a bubble but.

Commitment to action

Fill out the ROI matrix to identify and start prioritising your high-performing customers. Identify one strategy to train your customers and start using it. Identify one strategy to train your colleagues and start using it.

7

T Is For Train Hard, Fight Easy

BOTTOM LINE UP FRONT

Uncomfortable truth:

Being a trail-blazing uni-tasker isn't easy. You'll need to make some difficult decisions. But you can train yourself to do this. How you measure up under pressure is not something you're born with. It's something you learn, and it's something you can improve.

Business gains:

Better productivity and decision-making under pressure. Better ability to focus (even during confusion and stress).

Personal gains:

Feel more confident and calmer during difficulties.

It's training, not character

Warning: the following paragraphs contain potentially upsetting mental images. Skip this bit if you're scared of water. Or helicopters.

Imagine you are on a helicopter sightseeing trip in the Caribbean. The setting sun is casting a pink and golden glow across the shimmering horizon. The air is warm and tastes pleasantly salty on your tongue. You have left behind the white sandy beaches and are looking out over endless ripples of turquoise, greenish-blue and azure. The helicopter purrs gently.

And then the engine of the helicopter coughs. It coughs again. And then it's silent. Without warning, the aircraft yaws violently to the left. You are pinned to the side of your seat as your stomach simultaneously lurches to your chest. The helicopter is descending rapidly towards the sea. The ripples grow larger; you can make out the frothy peaks of the waves. Just as you are about to hit the sea, the helicopter floats, hanging in the air. You think, 'It's all going to be OK.' Then there's a deafening thud as the helicopter impacts the water.

Seconds later, water pours in through every cavity. The Caribbean Sea is pretty much like bathwater, but the force of it takes your breath away, and you involuntarily start to hyperventilate. It's almost at your chin when, once again, you are pinned to the side of the helicopter. You're aware you're rotating through an axis, but you're not sure which one. Everything is blurry. You become vaguely aware of the frenzied legs and arms of other passengers, but it's getting harder and harder to see... Because it's getting darker. You are sinking. Upside down. Strapped inside a metal cage.

I don't mean to unnecessarily traumatise you, but this is a possible scenario of what would happen if you ditched in a helicopter. My advice then is if you are thinking of going on a helicopter sightseeing tour, find a helicopter that has water skids or go dressed in full scuba gear. Do not kid yourself that if you ditched, you'd be ordained with a heroic sense of calm and would know exactly what to do. Instinct will not get you out alive.

I've been dramatic here for a reason. We need to ditch the narrative that how we respond under pressure is somehow a mark of our character. As I said in Habit H, it is not a mark of our character; it is a mark of our training. This is why we did underwater escape training (fondly referred to as 'the dunker'), because the sad but compelling truth is this: when a battle helicopter ditches, the only people who get out alive are the ones who have done dunker training.

Think about it – do you honestly believe the people who have survived ditching felt calm when they hit the water? Do you think they were any less afraid than you would be? Of course not. It was their training that kicked in. It was their training that saved them. It's the training that makes a difference when we are under pressure. And it's time you invested in yours.

I haven't shared this story out of some masochistic desire to put you off going in a helicopter. Flying in a helicopter is glorious and I highly recommend it (though, based on my tendency to crash, I might suggest choosing a different pilot). I've shared this story to make an important point about how we operate under pressure and, therefore, what we need to do to have a hope in hell of *uni-tasking* under pressure.

You may recall that when we are stressed, the rational evolved part of the brain gets bypassed and the automatic 'chimp' part of the brain starts running the show. It's hard to do new or complex things under pressure, no matter how much you try and will yourself to do it.

So, if you're waiting for the next time you're feeling overwhelmed and totally stressed out to *start* uni-tasking, it's not going to happen. Part of the reason for that is that we are not great at prioritising under pressure. Recall from Habit H that the brain goes into threat mode and defaults to assigning *everything* as urgent important (because it operates on a 'better safe than sorry' principle), which is why we covered some immediate actions we could use to get ourselves from fight or flight (totally freaking out) to 'healthy stress' so that we can prioritise effectively.

There is another step we can take, though, and it's worth it. You see, it *is* possible to uni-task under pressure, provided we work *with* the brain rather than against it. We do that by making uni-tasking automatic. If it's automatic, then even the chimp part of the brain can do it. And guess how we make something automatic? Repetition. During peacetime we train and train and train, so that when bullets fly over our heads, we don't have to think rationally; we already instinctively know what to do.

You can do the same. And you don't have to crash helicopters to do it. You just need to commit to uni-tasking on a regular and repeated basis. Spoiler alert: the easiest way to make sure you do something repeatedly is to make it part of your routine. Let's break it down with the 'train hard, fight easy' method.

Train Hard Part 1: Creating optimal conditions

We've established that training matters. It is the training you put in that will determine how effectively you can uni-task under pressure; and the more we repeat certain actions, the more automatic they are. But when I say train hard, I'm not suggesting that you need to uni-task on a bed of broken glass underneath a motorway bridge. You don't have to be a martyr to the cause. If you were training hard for your first-ever marathon, for example, you wouldn't run the entire route in bare feet, dressed as a deep-sea diver carrying a suitcase on your back. You'd make sure you had the right running shoes. You'd select your route carefully so that you didn't sprain an ankle on day one. You'd make sure your nutrition was supporting your running goals. In other words, you'd make the training as painless as possible so you can keep doing it. The same is true for uni-tasking. When I say train hard, I'm talking about the level of commitment we put in while curating the optimal conditions for training to assure success. So, the first bit of training is how to optimise the conditions for uni-tasking:

- First, write down your high-energy time of day, as identified in Habit B: this is the optimum time for you to uni-task.

- Next, write down where you will do this. Ideally, this is somewhere with minimum distractions.

- Finally, write down which tasks you will uni-task. Remember, not all tasks are created equal. Some tasks are meatier or require more motivation than others. Some tasks will be of higher value and have a greater impact on your desired outcomes. It's best to select the high-energy, high-impact tasks for uni-tasking, as this is how you can get the most out of your day.

Boom! Now you have your uni-tasking routine, but you also need to plan how you will protect this time. Think of this as creating your Focus Fortress.[36] I know this may sound like heresy, but you *can* turn your notifications off during this time. Most devices and platforms have 'focus' or 'do not disturb' modes, which you can programme according to the time of day. I've sold my soul to Apple, so I also programme my devices to go into uni-tasking mode whenever I open my keynote app (PowerPoint for everyone else) or whenever I'm on a Zoom call. I've also set this mode up so that only certain contacts can call me during this time.

Some people set up auto-replies on their emails to indicate when they are unavailable. You could start by closing down browsers and tabs that you don't need and putting your phone in the drawer. I've also heard great reports of a programme called Focusmate – this is a virtual space for people to work alongside a focus buddy.[37] One initiative I loved was the practice where people don their 'thinking caps'. In this instance, people would put a baseball cap on, and this would signal to everyone else that they are engaged in deep work and would prefer not to be interrupted.[38] Other people wear headphones to send the same signal. If you wear headphones, you can experiment with music such as binaural beats which are specifically designed to help you focus.

Take a minute to write down the protection measures you'll put in place to protect the time for your uni-tasking routine.

The purpose of all of the above is simple. It's to create the optimal conditions so that you can do uni-tasking repeatedly. This is how we make uni-tasking automatic and can, therefore, do it under pressure.

Note: even in optimal conditions, you will almost certainly get distracted from time to time. You could live a monastic existence surrounded by nothingness and your own wandering mind would find ways to sabotage you. Don't worry, this is normal. You don't have to become a guru from Headspace to achieve an epic level of focus. Simply practise refocusing your attention where you want it to be whenever you notice you've become distracted. You may even want to use your 'Fly the aircraft' hook that we discovered earlier. This is all covered in more detail in Habit A, so head back there if you'd like to refresh yourself at this point.

Remember, *every time* you notice you've become distracted and you refocus your attention where you want it to be, you're training your brain. You're training hard. It is a win-win scenario.

By the way, I said that the object is *not* to make the training difficult. The truth is, we don't need to. It will happen anyway, because of the way the modern world works and, in particular, the way other humans work. As we discussed in Habit I, other people will derail our best efforts to achieve a deep singular focus. No matter how great the above plan is, we can't eradicate the free will of other humans, and they will interrupt us. The majority of them will have bought into the culture that multi-tasking is a strength. They'll expect you to drop things for them, and it's *hard* to say no to them. But it's not impossible.

We covered some strategies for how to interact with other people in Habit I. In this section, though, I'm going to look at how we can train ourselves as individuals to have the gentle, but firm conversations that are often necessary. I'm going to look at how we can train ourselves to do things which are hard, but not impossible. I'm going to look at how we can train ourselves to do uncomfortable things. This is where the second part of 'train hard' comes in.

Train Hard Part 2:
Developing distress tolerance

We can all think of occasions where we've felt uncomfortable at work or in our business. Maybe we are waiting for a client to send back a signed contract. The hours stretch out, and the days seem endless. We start filling the time with overthinking: 'Maybe I got the wording slightly wrong in my last communication and I upset them? Maybe someone else has offered something more appealing? Maybe I should just send a little email to them? Come to think of it, there is another client who has gone quiet... Perhaps I'll send them an email at the same time, filling it with playful emojis to conceal my desperation. I simply can't tolerate this silence.'

Maybe your boss has asked you to work on an additional project. You're already pretty much at capacity, but you like your boss. And you really like having a job. Your boss encourages you to be honest about your workload and feed back if it's not achievable. But you don't want to be the person who actually takes them up on their offer and does the unthinkable: tells their boss the truth. That would be excruciatingly uncomfortable – it can't be done.

Maybe there is a colleague at work who is struggling to get to grips with a particular challenge. It's not actually your job to help, but you've talked them through a few bits to help them on their way. The thing is, they keep coming back to you. You know that you've given them all the information you can and suspect they would benefit from working through it themselves, but it's impossible to resist them when they look so helpless. You can't bear that sad look in their eyes.

That, right there, is why we end up multi-tasking. We take on more than is helpful and try to do it all at once because we tell ourselves the alternative is intolerable. We tell ourselves we have no choice. Wrong. We have a choice. It's just not an easy one.

The choice is to sit with difficulty. And to tolerate it. Even to lean in. And guess what? We can train ourselves to do this. This is what's known as 'distress tolerance'. Distress tolerance is a mindfulness technique that I learned when I trained to be a mindfulness coach. It might not sound like much fun, but it's key to increasing our confidence to handle difficult situations, feelings and thoughts. Remember the 'dunker' (the underwater escape training we do before we fly over the water)? It saves lives, but it's also terrifying, which is why it's the perfect way to demonstrate and practise distress tolerance.

CASE STUDY: Developing distress tolerance

I remember sitting on the side of the pool, consumed by fear. I didn't know what to do with this fear, so I did the only thing I could think of. I started gabbling: 'How long will I be underwater for? Has anyone died doing this? What if my harness gets caught? What happens if I get kicked in the face by a member of the crew and I pass out? What if the rescue diver doesn't notice…?'

I remember another helicopter pilot turning to me at this point and saying, 'Sarah, I get that you're scared. I'm scared, too.'

I looked at him disbelievingly. 'You don't seem very scared, I said.'

'Of course I'm scared, I just don't think talking about it is helping anyone.' I realised he was right. I had thought talking about it would calm me down. I was trying to rationalise it in my head, but actually, it was just fuelling my fear and driving everyone else around me mad. I decided to try doing what he was doing. I sat in meditative silence, letting myself feel whatever I needed to feel in the moment without fighting it or trying to rationalise it. I let the fear wash through me.

I thought to myself, 'I'm scared. And it's OK that I'm scared. And it's OK that I don't like being scared. But this is a feeling. I can tolerate it.' Do you know what happened? The tension started to dissolve. I began to feel slightly calmer and slightly more confident. I remember when I finally did the 'dunking'. I did, in fact, get caught up in the straps as I tried to get out. Rather than desperately trying to free myself like a trapped animal, I got back into my seat, reorientated, disentangled my straps, and then swam to safety. Afterwards, the safety diver had a look of total confusion on his face: 'I've never seen someone get back into their seat. It was like you had all the time in the world.'

That's the power of distress tolerance. When you stop fighting or fuelling your emotions and have the ability to sit with them as they are, they lose their power over you. The reason this is so effective is because emotions want to be heard – particularly uncomfortable emotions like fear or anxiety. That's because they are trying to protect you. If you try and eliminate them by ignoring them or by wrestling with them, they just shout louder. But if you can cultivate an ability to sit with a difficult feeling and just witness it, often that's all the emotion needs, and it will take care of itself. Here's a meditation you can do that will help you practise this.

EXERCISE: Sitting with difficulty meditation

Read through the following instructions several times or listen to the guided meditation on Soundcloud at https:// soundcloud.com/user-978445649 – 'Sitting with difficulty'. This meditation is a great way to train yourself to 'get comfortable being uncomfortable' and can increase your confidence dealing with challenges at work.

- Begin your meditation with your feet on the floor, bottom on the chair, relaxed but intentional posture, and softly lowered gaze or closed eyes.

- When you're ready, bring your attention to your breath. Notice each breath in and each breath out. Don't try and change it, just simply observe your breath.

- If you notice your attention has wandered to painful thoughts or feelings, allow the sensations to be present in your body without resisting them.

- If nothing has come to mind, try to recall a situation that has been causing you difficulty. It doesn't have to be anything major – just enough for the difficulty to come to mind now.

- Check in with how this uncomfortable experience shows up for you. What physical sensation occurs with these thoughts or emotions? What reaction do you have to these sensations? Do you notice any tendency to engage with these emotions – analysing, problem-solving, brooding?

- Now imagine, if you can, observing yourself in this moment. You might like to visualise yourself wherever you are sitting now, as if witnessing this moment from an out-of-body experience.

- See if you can visualise just sitting next to the version of you that is in pain and just witnessing that pain. There is nothing to say and no need to try and give an opinion or to take the pain away. It is simply enough to sit in companionable silence, acknowledging your pain.

- If you like, you might say, 'It's OK to feel like this. Whatever it is, it is OK to feel like this.'

- Now see if you can notice where in your body you feel this pain the most. You can rest your attention there for a while.

- Imagine breathing into and nourishing that part of the body and then exhaling and letting go of any tension that is there.

- When you notice the bodily sensations are no longer pulling so strongly for your attention, return your focus to your breath, remembering that you always have this as an anchor.

- When you are ready, you can open your eyes.

You may not feel inspired to meditate, or you may want something you can use in the heat of the moment when you are at work. In which case, try repeating this phrase in your head: *'This is uncomfortable, and it's OK that it feels uncomfortable. It's OK that I don't like feeling like this. I can tolerate it.'* And then, just do whatever that uncomfortable thing is. I like to refer to this as JFDI. I'll let you figure out what that means.

🔍 Why the juice is worth the squeeze

I'm not advocating that you sit with difficulty for hours on end. That's just self-sabotage and torture. The purpose of sitting with difficulty is to teach yourself that you *can* tolerate difficulty whenever it comes up. Every time you practise sitting with difficulty you are training your brain. You are teaching it, 'I can do difficult things. I can tolerate difficulty. And I can survive it.' And over time you will actually start to rewire your brain. And you will cultivate an inner confidence and a new belief: I can tolerate difficulty.

That means the next time you find yourself in an awkward situation (ie, you know deep down what you need to do, but it's deeply uncomfortable), you don't have to run away from it. You can lean into it.

The next time your boss says, 'Is now a good time?' steel yourself and say, 'Thank you for asking. I really want to do a great job on this piece of work, so I'll come and find you in twenty minutes if that works?' I know, right? That sentence feels terrifying to say. But in my experience, most people are pretty decent, and as long as you are polite, they can tolerate a bit of honesty. And so can you. Then, you will be free to do your best work, which you will do by giving it your full and undivided attention. This is ultimately how you serve others best.

Fight easy

A quick recap: we are not designed to come up with new or complex ways of doing things under pressure. It takes too long. We are designed to do what is automatic. So, if we want to do things well under pressure, they need to be automatic behaviours. And the easiest way to make something automatic is to do it repeatedly.

In this section, we've looked at two behaviours that are worthy of repetition: uni-tasking and sitting with difficulty. The outcomes of repeating these are:[39]

- Better ability and greater confidence to prioritise when we are overloaded

- Increased ability to focus more deeply and for longer, even among noise and distractions

- Feeling more confident protecting our boundaries and saying no to people when they turn the heat up

- Being able to hold our nerve in a vacuum of information rather than overthinking

It worth acknowledging that standing our ground with our boss or colleagues is going to feel uncomfortable. That's the point. The repetition of doing slightly uncomfortable things in optimal conditions is what allows us to do these things when the heat gets turned up. In other words, the training hard is what allows us to fight easy. Before you talk yourself out of it and say, 'Oh, I can't commit to all that training,' continue to keep in mind that *every time* you repeat an action, you increase your chances of being able to do it under pressure. The important thing is just to start. Even practising the behaviour just once is better than not doing it at all. And I can prove it.

CASE STUDY: A repeat incident

Two years after I hit the wires in Morocco I was flying down a very different valley. This one was in Wales. It was the southern entrance to the Wye Valley, just after you've crossed the impressively large Severn Bridge. Lessons had been learned from my previous experience in Morocco; I now understood that wires can be hard to spot, especially when you're flying in valleys, because the workload is high and the pylons that connect the wires can be concealed by vegetation.

I had made a point of studying the map so that I could apprise myself of all obstructions on our route. The valley was characterised by steep sides and sharp bends. In addition, it was a known area for fighter jets to fly. I knew from personal experience – I'd flown down it myself a few years earlier in a Hawk. We were keen not to meet a jet coming the other way, so we agreed we would hug the valley floor underneath the jet traffic. I was the navigating pilot, so I set to the task of briefing the flying pilot on what was coming up next, rather like those rally car drivers who have co-drivers talking them around the course. It was all going so well. And then…

'Fuck!' A crew member shouted a familiar cry. I didn't even see the wires. But I immediately knew, with a slightly sinking feeling, that we'd just hit them. Again.

Without a moment's hesitation, I selected the landing gear *down*, transmitted the radio call and completed the emergency landing checks.

Straight ahead was a grassy bank – a perfect spot for us to land – and we settled the aircraft down. After we landed, I marked the spot on the GPS and hit stop on the stopwatch (which is the terribly hi-tech way we had of measuring flight time back in those days).

'Total flight time – twenty-three minutes,' I said to the other pilot. We were safe and sound. A few days later, he came up to me and said, 'I can't get over how you did that. I was still processing what had just happened and you just cracked on and did everything! How did you do that?'

Of course, *you* know how I did it, don't you? You know why I was able to carry out the necessary immediate actions under pressure with such ease. Quite simply, it's because it wasn't my first time. I already knew exactly what to do in that moment – because I'd done it before.

The point is this stuff works. I may have learned uni-tasking in the cockpit, but these techniques are completely transferable into your daily routine, and you can train yourself to do these things under pressure by doing them repeatedly. You might surprise yourself at how effortless you make it look. People will regard you with awe. They'll assume you were born with superhero tendencies. But you'll know the truth is much more satisfying: you've earned it because you've learned it. Let me illustrate this with another story which doesn't involve crashing helicopters. It involves the commonplace, yet sometimes terrifying experience of going to school.

CASE STUDY: 'Instinctive' reactions

One day, as my twin and I left the school gates, we saw a gathering of children who looked unusually pleased to see us.

They were holding something in their hands. Then we realised – they were eggs. And we immediately understood that we were to be the chickens. We were to be chased the whole way home while they pelted eggs at us.

I remember this incident clearly. What I didn't remember until my sister pointed it out was what I'd yelled during our sprint home.

'Don't run in a straight line!' Miriam recalled. 'I'd never have thought of that, but it made total sense,' she said. 'I remember thinking, how does she know to do that? She must be really smart.'

Of course, I'd love to take the credit. I'd love to say I'm naturally smart, quick thinking and competent under pressure. But I know differently. The real reason I knew to run in a zig-zag was because I'd watched the war movie *Platoon* about seventeen times.[40] (I was a real tomboy back then and fancied myself as a bit of an action figure, plus I often get my best inspiration from movies: just look what happened after I watched *Top Gun*.) Truthfully, I don't remember watching the film and thinking, 'Next time I get eggs thrown at me, I'll run like Charlie Sheen.' It must have just lodged itself in my brain somewhere. But when it mattered, I 'instinctively' knew what to do.

So, it's a useful reminder: what we think of as instinct is actually a learned behaviour, and we learn through repetition. I repeat. We learn through repetition. And sometimes, we learn things in the most surprising ways. Remember this: our decisions and actions under pressure are the result of everything that has come before: the skills we've learned, the knowledge we have acquired, the practice of focusing on one thing at a time, the practice of refocusing if we get distracted and the practice of sitting with difficulty.

Key takeaways

- The key to uni-tasking, or doing anything well under pressure, is to make it automatic. The key to making something automatic is repetition. The key to repetition is routine.

- 'Train hard' doesn't mean becoming a martyr. It means putting in the work under optimal conditions. We can create optimal conditions for uni-tasking by minimising distractions and clearly signalling to others when we need to work uninterrupted.

- Minimising disruptions from others will require a willingness to have uncomfortable conversations. We can train ourselves to feel more confident during uncomfortable situations.

Commitment to action

Write down and commit to your uni-tasking routine. Put it up somewhere visible or share it with your work colleagues (getting ready for Habit S). Identify your optimal uni-tasking conditions and identify three changes you could make to your environment to make these easier. Try practising the 'sitting with difficulty' meditation three times this week (informal or formal).

8

S Is For Set The Conditions

BOTTOM LINE UP FRONT

Uncomfortable truth:

The biggest thing that will get in your way is you. The biggest thing that will get in other people's way is you. Your solution is not the only solution. Great leadership is about creating the space for people to love your idea and interpret and act on it in their own way.

Business gains:

Multiply productivity, reduce stress and increase retention.

Personal gains:

Stop fighting with the world. Start working with the world.

Set an example

OK. You are now a uni-tasking trailblazer. Give yourself a high-five. Or if that's too much, an inner smile. The next step is to share it with the people you work with. Or, in the case of solopreneurs, share it with your collaborators or suppliers. That means not only will their productivity soar and their stress decrease, which is great for you, your business and your life, but it'll also make it a hell of a lot easier for you to uni-task when they 'get it', which is even greater for you, your business and your life! But where do you start? Don't worry. I've got a plan for you.

Have you ever uttered these words about your parents?

'I'll never be like that.' Me too. Have you ever had that moment where you've realised: 'Shit, I'm just like them.' Me too. This is evidence of the power of example. No matter how much we try to fight it, we are inevitably influenced by the people around us, particularly the people we respect. Whether unconsciously or not, most people respect their parents.

The good news is that even if it's subconscious, the people we surround ourselves with also respect us. They will follow our example, even if they don't think they want to or realise this is what they are doing. I talk about this in the 'campaign of influence' in Chapter 9.

So, even if you do nothing else except start uni-tasking yourself and setting a great example for others, you'd be off to a superb start. You just have to start. But you're a trailblazer. Trailblazers don't just tread a path that hasn't been trodden before; they forge a path for others to follow. This means we need to look at how we can make it easy for others to uni-task. What we do is set the conditions for others to follow our example.

Setting the conditions for others

The good news is you've done some of the hard work already. Remember in Habit T when you wrote down the measures to help create and protect the optimal conditions for uni-tasking? I referred to it as the 'focus fortress'. Well, if you want people to follow your example, it might just be helpful for others to have a focus fortress, too.

A great starting point is to write down your protective measures from Habit T and work out how to make these accessible as common working practices for those in your team, ie, 'Common working practices that I would like to facilitate (so people can follow my example).'

Then it's worth thinking about what you need to do to enable people to put these working practices into... Well, practice. For example, you might decide to have a comms-free window while you're uni-tasking, where you are not going to answer your emails. Consider what your team need from you to feel confident implementing the same policy. Maybe they need to know they've got your blessing to have a response time of an hour (as opposed to, you know, nine seconds). Or, if you've identified a quiet zone where you can work uninterrupted, consider how you could make a quiet zone available for everyone.

Remember, though, we are all different. We all have slightly different ways of working. We have different energy peaks throughout the day. Some achieve their best focus in the humdrum of an open-plan office. Others need to completely shut themselves off from outside noises. So, a great idea at this point is to speak to the people in your team and find out what they need in order to uni-task effectively. First of all, though, they need to know what uni-tasking is and decide to buy into it. This is where we can have a bit of fun.

Sharing the uni-tasking 'secret'

My top tip here: don't try and sell uni-tasking to them. People don't like being told what to do, especially if it involves effort and a change in behaviour. And they definitely don't like being told what to think, but you can create the space for them to start thinking positively about uni-tasking. The best way to do this? Divulge the information like it's your best-kept secret. It really bloody works.

I can remember the exact moment I learned about plate tectonics. I didn't learn it from a teacher or a textbook. A school friend leaned in conspiratorially and said, 'Have you ever noticed that the east coast of South America fits perfectly into the west coast of Africa?' I was stunned. I replied in earnest, 'Do you think anyone else has noticed?' It turns out this school friend had just learned about Pangea in geography.

There are three steps to divulging the information:

1. **Share your 'secret':** You could open with: 'Did you know that multi-tasking is a myth? Our attention can only be in one place at a time, so when we're multi-tasking, what we're doing is task switching.' I can remember the first time someone shared this with me. I was about twenty-two years old, and we were in flying training at the time. 'So, it turns out it's better to focus on *one* thing at a time and give that your full attention.' I felt like I had just been trusted with top-secret information, not dissimilar to the way I felt when I'd 'discovered' Pangea.

2. **Give them time to see the awesomeness of the 'secret':** Now you wait for them to decide they'd like

to try it, too. My advice: don't force this. If they're not ready to follow your example, just keep doing what you're doing. Keep being mega-productive and infuriatingly Zen and don't be afraid to signpost what you are doing. For example, when they interrupt you when you are uni-tasking, you can deploy one of the responses from Habit I: 'I can see this is important and deserves my full attention... Shall we chat about it between X and Y?' They'll catch on. And when they do...

3. **Allow them to 'steal' your secret:** When they come to you and express an interest in uni-tasking, you can say: 'If you want to uni-task, I can support that. Since I've started uni-tasking, I've noticed there are some things that can make it easier, like turning off notifications. What about you? What do you think would make it easier for you to uni-task?'

Another 'secret' you can share is about high-energy times of your day/week. Here's a possible template: 'Did you know they studied judges to determine what most influenced the leniency of parole sentences? The biggest causal factor that determined how lenient they were was how long it had been since they'd last had a break.[41] So, basically, our energy and motivation to do good work are finite resources. And they ebb and flow throughout the day. We are more productive if we do our high-value tasks when we have a high amount of energy and motivation.'

Once you've planted the seed, they might start to become more aware of their high-energy time of day... And their low-energy time of day. Remember, keep the faith, and keep signposting what you are doing – for example, 'I'm going to tackle this task first thing tomorrow, because I know that's when I'll give it my first team energy.'

Enabling others to steal this secret is an easy one. You just have to show an interest and ask questions like, 'What's your best time of day?' In my experience, people love answering this question. They get enthusiastic sharing their high-energy time of day:

- 'I have to do my most important job as soon as I walk through the door!'

- 'Oh no, I need to clear my inbox first, so I have a clear mind.'

- 'Speak for yourself. I'm a 3 am-er.'

- 'You're all wrong. I'm most productive at 4 pm on Friday.'

- 'I'm only really productive when the kids are in bed.'

Don't worry if people get a bit protective of their best time of day. It shows they're invested in the idea. And then, boom, they're invested in making the most of this period. It's almost like it's their idea. Then, you can ask a few more questions: 'Which tasks do you think need your first team energy? What needs to be in place to help you make the most of your high-energy time of day?'

I've done multiple workshops with the 'secret' method, and it's revealed great results. One of the simplest but most effective secrets was this: 'Did you know that *not* everything is equally important?' Once you've planted the seed, they might start to reflect on the times they've assumed something was world-endingly important, only to realise a few hours or days later it really wasn't that important after all. Now, they are giving themselves permission to prioritise. You've done them a *huge* favour. They may say, 'I thought about what you said, and I agree. But how can I tell in the moment what's not as important?' At which point, you reply, 'You're right. It *is* hard at the moment. I find I prioritise better when I'm feeling calm. I have a little system I use to help me prioritise more effectively. I can talk you through it if you like.' At this point, you could refer to Habits H or B.

☾ Why the juice is worth the squeeze

You might notice something about HABITS. It's all about using influence to achieve a change in behaviour. You could say it's manipulative, but I think it's a skilful and emotionally intelligent way of helping people discover their own motivation for making positive change. You can order people around as much as you like. Trust me, I did plenty of that in the military. But when I left the military, I learned how to become a coach, and it opened my eyes to a far more skilful way to lead, live and run my business.

This is important, because you cannot force people to love your idea, but you can create the space for them to fall in love with it through their own free will. Plant the idea, share the information generously, and then let people find their own motivation to follow your example. In my opinion, there is nothing more powerful than harnessing intrinsic motivation.

Getting out of the way

You've set the example. You've made it as easy as you can for others to follow your example. And now you're ready for the final piece of the puzzle, which is making sure you don't sabotage all your good work by getting in everyone's way. There is a fun exercise you can do to bring this to life. It's called the reverse brainstorm (BS).

EXERCISE: Reverse BS

Start with a positive question: 'How could I make it easier for others to uni-task?'

Then reverse the question: 'How could I make it harder for others to uni-task?' Brainstorm the most ludicrous ways you could make it harder for people. (Get the people in your team involved if you want to think big here.) Common examples include:

- Being a bubble but.

- Micromanaging people.

- Expecting everyone to drop everything for your top priority. (Remember, don't confuse collaboration with duplication – high-performing teams can work on complementary priorities.)

- Giving vague direction about the end goal so people can't prioritise.

- Bollocking people if they act with a degree of autonomy and get it slightly wrong. If you empower people to be self-sufficient and to push themselves, you need to give them the freedom to learn from trial and error, too.

- Being offended if people say, 'Actually, I'm in the middle of something – could I come back to you shortly.'

- Expecting everyone to work exactly the same way you work.

- Championing uni-tasking and then telling everyone they need to have an open-door policy at all times.

Now you've got a load of ideas of what *not* to do. Reverse them. You've got some great working practices. I could sum them up like this: practise what you preach. Don't be a dick. This is also a great exercise to do with your team. Once they've started to buy in (after the 'secret' phase), you can ask them, 'What would make it easier for you to uni-task? Actually, let's have some fun with this. What would make it harder for you to uni-task?' This works for several reasons. Remember, we don't like change; it's scary, and it takes effort. So, we are *really* good at finding reasons not to do things. This exercise allows us to work with the brain instead of against it. It allows us to embrace our 'negative Nellie' streak as a force for good.

If you're the boss, chances are people will find it hard to say, 'I find it really hard to focus when you're continually asking for updates.' Yet, time and again, when I give talks to big corporates, the CEO or MD will stand up afterwards and say, 'I see now I can be a bit of a bubble but. I'm going to change that.' If the boss can admit it, it paves the way for others to recognise when they, too, can be disruptive to others. But even better, they're reducing the fear people might experience over giving a bit of feedback if they demonstrate they can admit when they are wrong. So, the reverse BS exercise is essentially you 'going first'. You're giving people the space to say things they might not usually have the courage to say to you. By taking it on the chin, you're demonstrating your commitment to them. And the chances are they'll be even more committed to you and the change initiative as a result. It might sting a bit, of course. But you've got this.

Key takeaways

- It's a powerful moment when the boss can show a bit of vulnerability.

- Sharing information like it's a secret is a superb way to spark interest. It also makes it a bit more fun for you.

Commitment to action

Proactively create the space for others to follow the path you have blazed. Encourage commitment by giving people the opportunity to be honest with you.

PHASE THREE

CREATE A UNI-TASKING CULTURE

Now it's time to put everything you've learned into practice, deal with whatever gets in the way and begin uni-tasking your way to success. Mega fist-bump moment.

9

The Role Of Leadership
In Uni-tasking

BOTTOM LINE UP FRONT

Uncomfortable truth:
It takes more than just knowing what to do.
It takes leadership.

Business gains:
Increase the productivity of your whole workforce.

Personal gains:
Discover your ability to be a force for good.

You're already a leader

I want to take a moment now to sprinkle a bit of fairy dust on the HABITS method and to explain the DNA that is woven through this book. It comes down to one word: leadership.

The method I have shared is uni-tasking. But the way to implement that method takes self-leadership and, if you run a team, leadership of others. For this reason, you will have found references to leadership throughout this book. Because if you want to change your habits, and if you want to be an agent for change for others, it takes leadership. You might be thinking, 'But I am no leader!' (Answer: you are already more of a leader than you probably give yourself credit for.) Or, 'But I'm a solopreneur, what has leadership got to do with me?' Or, 'Why is Sarah trying to make this about leadership when she told me to focus on *one* thing at a time?' (Good point: I'll answer this fully below.)

Why is leadership important to the implementation of uni-tasking? There are a few reasons. One of them is that the world at large still believes that multi-tasking is a fabulous idea, so you'll be swimming against the stream when you start uni-tasking. That means you will need to make a decision to forge your own path rather than waiting for others to do it for you. That's leadership.

As I said above, you're probably already better at this leadership stuff than you give yourself credit for. Take a moment now to reflect on all the moments today you've decided to do something without being told to do it by someone else, for example:

- Deciding when to go to the gym

- Deciding what to eat for lunch

- Deciding which route to take to work

Your decisions may well have been influenced by other factors, but, ultimately, you made a decision. You took the lead in your own life. That's all I'm asking you to do with uni-tasking. Don't wait to be told. Take the lead. 'Fly your aircraft.'

Leading others

Let's look at why leadership of others is important. Leadership can mean different things to different people; it is generally defined as 'the action of leading a group of people'. I've spent many years fascinated by leadership and here's my current[42] best approximation of what 'good leadership' means to me: 'Leading the way by doing stuff that others find too difficult or scary for a cause beyond our own.'

I won't go into detail as to how I arrived at this approximation. I give whole speeches about this and I won't attempt to summarise them here (and besides, this book is about uni-tasking, not leadership). All I'll say is that leading the way in uni-tasking fits this description: uni-tasking is difficult and scary for others to do for a number of reasons, many of which we explored in Phase One. It will also hugely benefit others if they start uni-tasking (for reasons we explored in Phase One).

Let me be clear about one thing. *Everyone* is a leader. Leadership happens at all levels of a business and in all walks of life. Whether you're a business owner, a manager, a solopreneur, a parent, mentor or role model, you're leading the way for more people than you'll probably ever give yourself credit for. So, it's worth understanding this stuff.

This next section explains the leadership ideology which is infused into HABITS, and I'm talking about leadership of change in particular. Because change will be required for most people (including you – well done for being brave) in order to implement uni-tasking. And leading through change requires what I like to call a 'campaign of influence'.

You may recall from Habit S that we cannot force people to love uni-tasking any more than we can force them to love change. We can *influence* how they think about it, though. We do that by going below the waterline of observed behaviours and influencing what is in people's heads – perhaps even before they know it themselves. By creating a space where every individual can be an autonomous, proactive and confident team member who thinks like a leader, who is as invested as a business owner and who has the self-belief to see things through. By changing the way people think, feel and, ultimately, what they believe in order to effect meaningful and lasting positive change – not to serve our own ends, but to make things better for them.

Consider: do you want people to be more proactive and reduce the tendency to delegate upwards, for example? You can't simply order them to stop delegating upwards. You can't tell them to take more initiative. Well, you can, but good luck getting them to buy in – what other people think is their prerogative and their privilege. We cannot force people to think differently, and nor should we. Not only is it disempowering; it's usually a waste of time. So, if we want people to be more proactive, we ultimately need them to think differently about their remit, their ability, their motivation and the repercussions of action and inaction.

The key to lasting and positive change is to change how people think, but we can't control how people think. So, how on earth do we achieve a campaign of influence? You can see why many people don't bother. A campaign of influence requires emotional intelligence, accountability, maturity and, above all, an appetite to play the long game and do what is genuinely right by others rather than ticking boxes – but I promise you, it works. Let me talk you through it.

You might find some of what follows feels oddly familiar – that's because these phases have been ingrained through the entire HABITS process. So, if you've been implementing HABITS, then you've been leading. See, I told you, you're already a leader.

The three phases to a campaign of influence

Let's take an example of a campaign of influence, which has the objective of promoting business growth:[43]

- Phase 1: Understand (30%)

- Phase 2: Influence (40%)

- Phase 3: Set the conditions (30%)

The percentages represent how much attention I will give to these stages and, therefore, how you should distribute your efforts to be the most effective leader. It's important to recognise that this is the opposite of 'old-guard style' leadership. I grew up with the notion that leadership was all about being the one at the front giving orders (ie, this style of leadership was almost exclusively about Phase 3: Set the Conditions), which is exactly why it has reduced effect. It's ignoring the 70% of what good leadership is constructed of, but that's about to change. When you focus your efforts on the 70%, not only does leadership become easier, it also becomes more enjoyable. And as an added bonus, that means you'll be 70% more effective than all the leaders out there who haven't read this book.

Phase 1: Understand

The object of this phase is to understand why people might have negative or unhelpful ideas about an initiative. These ideas will hold them back from implementing this initiative, so it will take extraordinary amounts of willpower and goodwill for them to bother. That is going to make your job as a leader exponentially more difficult, so a crucial place to start is to understand what people's barriers are so you know what you're up against. Then you'll have a fighting chance of working through these barriers.

To understand others, often the easiest place to start is ourselves. Ultimately, we are all human and are driven by the same thing: survival. So, during the Understand phase you could ask ourselves, 'Why might I resist uni-tasking?' (You might recall we did this through the Five Whys exercise.) I'll tell you my reasons for resisting uni-tasking (but please don't tell on me, I have a reputation to uphold):

- It takes effort to stay focused on one thing.

- I forget to uni-task when I've got a million things going on.

- Being able to focus on just one thing seems too good to be true.

- It suggests that something is wrong with the way I'm currently doing things.

- I'm scared that I'll prioritise the wrong thing.

- Nobody else seems to be doing it, so why am I bothering?

- I'm worried that people will find me anti-social or uncaring when I'm uni-tasking.

Understanding our own reasons can give us a lot of insight into why others might resist uni-tasking, too. It's a lot easier to muster patience and empathy for others who are most likely held back by similar thoughts.

It's also helpful to understand the science behind these thoughts. The fact I always come back to, is that we are wired for survival. For example, the brain doesn't like being confronted with unfamiliarity or uncertainty because it doesn't have an established behaviour to fall back on that has been proven to work. And if we don't know that it will work, then there's a chance we will die. In other words, unfamiliarity and uncertainty feel like a threat to life.

Add to this that at some point, we evolved to be tribal because there is safety in numbers. Therefore, we feel a primal urge to be liked and accepted as part of the tribe, which means we worry all the time about being rejected or looking stupid. So, we are loath to stick our heads above the parapet.

By spending time on the Understand phase, we can really get a handle on *why* people think the way they do. This is not so we can create excuses for poor behaviour, but so we can make it safe for people to make an important realisation: our biggest barrier is usually our own assumptions and learned thinking patterns. In other words, our biggest barrier is ourselves. And that's not because we are weak or lazy. It's because we are human.

When we combine all these factors, we create an environment in which we can understand the barriers to growth without judgement, which is great news, because if we can put them up, then we can also take them down.

Another crucial part of the Understand phase is to appreciate the science behind uni-tasking and the mindset that is required to embrace the challenges and implement positive, meaningful changes in our process. It is normal to revert to a more fixed mindset, particularly when it comes to change. This is the idea that we are the finished product and, 'I don't need to change anything, thank you very much. Who are you to tell me otherwise?' So, it's natural to expect a bit of resistance, which isn't a sign that uni-tasking is a lost cause. It's just a sign we are human and frightfully protective of familiarity.

The good news is that it's also human nature to keep striving and to find dissatisfaction with the status quo. This is why we often feel like we are not enough. It's why we might experience a bit of imposter syndrome. It's also why we evolve. There is nothing 'wrong' with us, then, for having a bit of imposter syndrome. In fact, it can provide motivation and fuel for continuous improvement. And there is nothing wrong with being a work in progress. In fact, we can learn to embrace it.

There's a wonderful thing called neuroplasticity, which means that the brain is capable of creating new neural pathways. Indefinitely. This means we can learn new behaviours, new thought patterns and even new emotional responses. It is literally *never* too late to teach an old dog new tricks. So, there is no need to worry about not being the finished article, perfect as we are. We have been blessed with the possibility of infinite self-improvement.

Phase 2: Influence by setting the example (operating within our circle of influence)

Now that we've understood the barriers and the reasons for them, and know that it's possible to remove them, we can move on to Phase 2. In order for this phase to work best, we need to have a good understanding of Covey's Circles of Influence and Concern.[44] Remember, we can't force people to think differently. What people think falls within our circle of concern. But we can be a positive influence (our circle of influence) and others will follow.

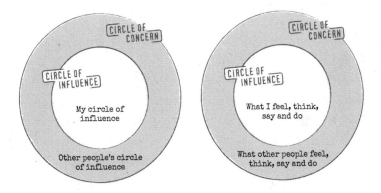

The Circles of Influence and Concern

By far the most effective way to influence others is to set an example. It is the simplest and most effective influence tactic in the book, yet it is so often overlooked. Yes, I know we often parrot the phrase 'lead by example', but how often do we actually do that? When we do decide to practise what we preach, though, it's astonishing how powerful it is. As proof of the sheer power of leading by example, I encouraged you earlier to think about your parents.

How many times when you were growing up did you think to yourself, 'When I grow, I'll never do that...' only to grow up and realise that you are doing exactly what they did? If you're like me, you might have wrestled with this. My God, did I fight the idea that I would be anything like my mother. My siblings and I, when we bickered, would throw poison darts in the form of, 'You're just like her,' because we knew how much it would hurt. I was desperate to be different. The thought of becoming my mum appalled me. (Sorry, Mum, I see now I was an idiot because you're actually bloody fabulous.) And yet, I'm just like her. Proof that no matter how much we fight it, we follow the example we are set.

There's a good reason for optimism here, though. I recently learned about the rule of three, which is a bit like the 'Six Degrees of Kevin Bacon' game (the idea that no matter which actor you name, they can all be linked back to Kevin Bacon in less than six connections). Well, the rule of three is similar in that it uses the inevitable interconnectedness of humans as a force for good. Simply put, if you show up as your best, with a growth mindset, you positively influence the three people next to you. And *they* positively influence the three people next to them. And *they* positively influence the three people next to them. This is exactly as Covey predicted.

An incredibly easy way to set an example is by choosing our narrative and making it growth-orientated. For example:

- Instead of saying, 'I can't play the piano,' we can say, 'I can't play the piano *yet*.'

- Instead of saying, 'I hate giving presentations,' we can say, 'I find presenting challenging.'

- Instead of saying, 'I should have asked for advice,' we can say, 'I could have asked for advice.'

- Instead of saying, 'I am enough,' we can say, 'I'll be OK.'

Try these phrases out and pay attention to how you feel about growth and yourself. You may notice that you start to feel just a little bit more confident and start to think a little bit more positively. Other people will notice that, too, and they'll want what you've got. Which means they'll start mimicking you, and they, too, will start thinking differently.

Phase 3: Set the conditions (for others to operate within their circle of influence)

This is where we start to truly master Covey's circles of concern and influence, because this stage is all about setting the conditions for others to grow within their circle of influence.

Remember, we cannot force people to love uni-tasking, prioritisation, change, uncertainty, failure, etc (all of which will be part of the journey – it's not called a 'hero's journey' for nothing). So, Phase 3 involves understanding where our circle of influence ends, and where someone else's starts. Because our circle of concern is someone else's circle of influence, and it's about respecting what is in other people's circle of influence (ie, the rate other people adapt to new ideas), or how other people see and value themselves. And then we set the conditions so that they can operate healthily and confidently within their circle of influence. So, really, Phase 3 is about getting out of other people's way.

When we think about setting conditions, I often start by asking myself the question, 'How do I create the space for them to (insert objective)?' Let's take the objective of growth, which is fundamental to adopting uni-tasking. In Phase 3, we can create the conditions for them to grow at their own pace. For that to happen, they need the space to do their own learning. Because we learn by making mistakes, we can demonstrate that it's OK for people to make mistakes. We can show them it's OK to admit to their mistakes. We can create the space for them to take responsibility for their mistakes.

Creating optimal conditions

All of these tactics mean we are making the conditions as optimal as possible for others to work within their circle of influence in a growth-orientated way. In my experience, if you give people the trust and the space to operate like this, you will be rewarded for the simple reason that most people, when it boils down to it, want to do their best and they want to please you. All we need to do as leaders is get out of their way and create the space for them to get out of their own way.

Of course, this requires a leap of faith and can sometimes appear counter-productive. Remember, no matter how inspirational you are as a leader, no matter how well you execute a campaign of influence, everyone still gets to choose what they think, and if they want to stay stuck in a fixed mindset, they will. That's the bummer of free will. But take heart: a campaign of influence doesn't need to change the mindset of every single person immediately. In fact, according to the 'Rule of Three', you only need one in three people to engage with this style of leadership in the first instance.

And the rest will follow. Just give it time. I promise you that a campaign of influence is not soft. It's bloody genius. And it works.

Key takeaways

A campaign of influence (and the leader's journey) follows three steps:

1. Know thyself.

2. Get out of your own way.

3. Get out of other people's way.

Commitment to action

Allow people to start thinking for themselves in a growth-minded way and your organisation will become more proactive, more cohesive, more creative and more resilient. The more we operate in our circle of influence, the bigger it gets.

10

Now Fly Your Aircraft (And Stay On Course)

BOTTOM LINE UP FRONT

Uncomfortable truth:

There will be times you feel like you're not making any progress.

Business gains:

Improved endurance and a growth mindset culture.

Personal gains:

Increased satisfaction and control.

Overcoming expectation barriers

It's not uncommon when I run workshops to see how people expend great effort finding all the reasons it's just too difficult to uni-task. I think, 'If only they could start with acceptance that progress is rarely found by taking the easy path and invest that effort in finding ways to make it easier, they'd already be making progress.' It does, however, shed light on the three biggest mindset barriers that kill progress:

1. Expectation of others

2. Expectation of immediacy

3. Expectation of satisfaction

Let's look at each more closely.

Expectation of others

Remember the Five Whys exercise from earlier? I asked you to think of your own personal barriers to uni-tasking. I also asked you to keep it in I-language. The reason for this is simple. We don't control what other people do. So, we are better off focusing on what we can change, which is… Ourselves.

If you want to start being more productive and less stressed, you need to take charge of the things in your circle of influence. That said, it's human nature to drift into our circle of concern. It's easy to see all the reasons why other people are the problem. So, if you notice you're veering off into your *circle of concern*, don't be too hard on yourself. Just gently escort yourself back into your circle of influence.

Be prepared for those around you to do the same. They'll start complaining about others or saying things like, 'I don't have a choice.' Be prepared to gently escort them back into their circle of influence. 'OK, so what can you control?'

Full disclosure: you might need to do this repeatedly. The circle of concern is seductive.

Expectation of immediacy

If you start uni-tasking, I expect you to see an improvement in your productivity. I'd also expect you to feel less overwhelmed, and I'd expect you to notice these improvements immediately. It is *that* magic. But the rest of the world... Well, it might take a little longer to catch up (see the point above – free will is a bummer sometimes).

Be prepared for the temptation to throw your arms up in the air at this point and think, 'Why can't they just get it already? They are derailing my amazing initiative!' That's understandable. But remember, it's their choice to fall in love with uni-tasking and establish the necessary boundaries and procedures to enable it. You don't control others. But you don't rely on them either.

So, keep doing what you're doing, enjoy your personal and immediate advantages, and play the long game with the people around you. They'll see the light eventually. This is one of the reasons I talk to schools about uni-tasking. The kids in Year 8 aren't going to be my employees any time soon, but if I can plant the idea (remember it's a *secret*), then we'll start to replace the multi-tasking narrative with the uni-tasking narrative. Bit by bit, we can change the world and make it better. It's evolution, not revolution.

Expectation of satisfaction

When I joined the RAF, people joked about women drivers, lumpy jumpers, and 'her indoors'. They rejected any expression of emotion with, 'Man up, wet pants!' We thought leadership was about being the most dominant voice in a room of 'like-minded' people.

When I left twenty-one years later, it was dramatically different. The mindset is now much more inclusive. Men now take six months of paternity leave. Women serve in the infantry. People talk openly about burnout and depression. We know the best teams are made up of people who are different: gender, background, education and neurodiversity. We talk about 'psychological safety' and we practise 'just culture'. If our idea of leadership, culture, mindset, failure and success is continually evolving, how can we ever really feel completely satisfied? By the time we get to be 'better', the thinking will have moved on... For the better.

This applies to uni-tasking, too. I believe in it. But my understanding of it is evolving. For example, I remember after a speech,[45] a girl asked, 'How does this apply to people with ADHD? We get bored easily and work better when we can task switch.'

I replied, 'Many of us get bored easily – this isn't a challenge exclusively for those with ADHD. The brain is completely trainable and practising mindfulness will help you to refocus when you get distracted.'

She shook her head. 'I tried mindfulness, but it doesn't work.'

I wanted to double down. However, I realised that this would be counter-productive and would inhibit progress. After all, we are no longer satisfied that all children learn the same way. We now understand we have different learning styles (my son has dyslexia, so I can relate). If we are no longer satisfied with the current schooling system in the UK, this might not feel like progress. But the fact that we are no longer satisfied proves that we have made progress. It shows that our understanding and thinking have moved on. That's why I've been researching uni-tasking strategies that are helpful for those with ADHD.[46]

By the way, this is not a get-out clause. I'm not trying to make excuses for the lack of progress. You can gauge progress in various ways. While our thinking is always evolving, we can still expect to find a higher degree of satisfaction through uni-tasking. For the simple reason that uni-tasking allows us to work smarter, not harder, it's probably the most important thing you can do to create a happier workforce.[47]

In summary, keep the faith. The changes you are making will make an impact, even if you won't realise it at the time, or if the people around you don't appreciate it. That's why it takes courage to do this stuff.

Key takeaways

- People will expend great effort finding all the reasons why it's too difficult to uni-task. The three biggest mindset barriers that kill progress are the:

    - Expectation of others

    - Expectation of immediacy

    - Expectation of satisfaction

- Uni-tasking allows you to work smarter, not harder.

Commitment to action

'Fly your aircraft' and stay on course.

Conclusion

I wrote this book for people with a high level of ambition who want to achieve great results without driving themselves into the ground. We live in a world where we are increasingly expected to do more with less, and we increasingly expect more of ourselves. The good news is that there really is a way to do this. Not only is it possible, but it could also make your life easier.

Let's remind ourselves how we do this: focus on *one* thing at a time. Or, in my world, 'Fly the aircraft'.

I'm not the first person to write a book about this. Indeed, I've drawn on some great resources such as *The One Thing* by Gary Keller and Jay Papasan and *Deep Work* by Cal Newport.[48] Actually, the list goes on. The point is, I'm not making this shit up. A lot of clever people have said the same things I'm saying. This is not new information, but it is information that we may have forgotten in this busy, 'now, now, now' world that we live in.

This is your reminder. It's the nudge to rediscover what you already knew deep down. Admit it. Nobody really believes they can do things better when they multi-task – not sensible people, anyway. This is your way to get back into uni-tasking, because habit is a killer when it's an unhelpful one. (Obviously, it's fabulous if it's helpful.)

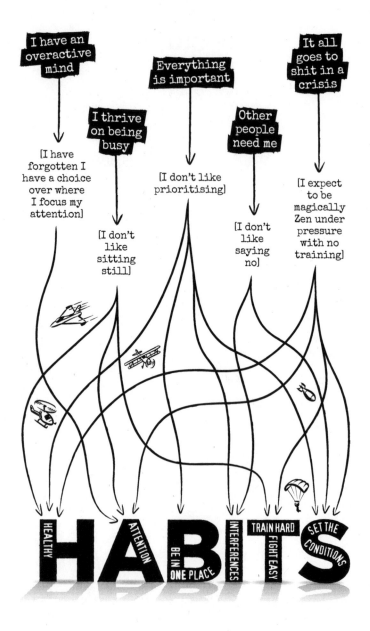

The HABITS method

If you've been multi-tasking for the last twenty years, it's going to be a little daunting unpicking all that. I get it. This HABITS method is my way of walking you through the journey to uni-tasking nirvana step by step. I've used experiences from my flying training, mindfulness coaching and all the way through to running a business single-handedly. So, I know this stuff works. And hopefully it's entertained you a little bit on the way.

I made it into a mnemonic so you can use it as a handrail going forward. My hope is that you can use it to educate others, and we can help spare the world from unnecessary burnout. Let's revisit everything you have achieved through the HABITS method.

First, you have to be in the right mental state to do effective work:

Healthy: You learned that we are crap at prioritising when we are totally maxed out (no, we do *not* thrive on stress), and we just end up adding a load of stuff to our to-do list, which further maxes us out. Habit H shows us how to recognise when we are maxed out and self-soothe.

Attention: Even if we are feeling calm, our monkey brains love to wander off. So, we learned how to refocus our attention every time we get distracted. The great news is every time we bring our focus back to where we want it to be, we are training our brains to achieve greater focus. We can also use this technique to use our attention as a force for good (ie, focus on your 'Fly the aircraft' priority and not what that nincompoop Bob said to you three days ago – it's really not worth your attention).

Now that you're in the right mindset, you can start uni-tasking and achieve higher performance while completing the tasks quickly:

Be in one place: Not all tasks are created equal. Some are more important than others, and important tasks are *not* always urgent, though the brain loves to trick us into thinking they are. In this section, I shared my step-by-step process for prioritising your tasks *and* planning to do them during your optimal windows of focus. And that's all very well until the outside world gets involved. And by that, I mean other people. Whether they are the people you work for (clients) or the people you work with (colleagues), I like to refer to them as interferences, because they all have one thing in common: they interfere with our flow. There is a way of protecting your uni-tasking bubble without losing all your top customers and pissing off your colleagues/friends/family.

Interferences: Not all clients are created equal. Perhaps if you're starting out in business, you'll be like I was – just so goddamn grateful for anyone who showed an interest. It took me a while to spot the clients who were draining more from me than they were giving. When you find the courage to discard these time-wasters, you can give your full attention to your high-value clients. That's a much easier way to do business, in my view. Habit I also looked at ways to train our colleagues and those around us to be more self-sufficient. This isn't mean. People are more capable than we think. We can create the conditions for uni-tasking by showing them that.

Next, you're ready to turn up the heat (ie, uni-task when the going gets tough):

Train hard, fight easy: Remember, I said we do *not* thrive on stress. But we can train ourselves to do things under pressure by making those actions automatic. How do we do that? Repetition. And what's the easiest way to repeat behaviours? Make them part of our routine. Commit to uni-tasking every day; then you'll have it to fall back on when the stress levels go up.

Now, the student becomes the master, which means you're ready to share this with the rest of the world:

Set the conditions: If you run a team of people, then by now, you'll probably appreciate how much everyone could benefit from uni-tasking. So, how do you get others to buy in? Simple. Start uni-tasking. Enjoy the plethora of benefits it bestows you. People catch on quickly. They'll follow your lead. You can share your wisdom to speed up the process (using the 'secret' formula). And then, finally, don't get in other people's way when they decide to uni-task. And if all else fails, just don't be a bubble but.

You've arrived at HABITS. The mnemonic is your step-by-step guide to building the uni-tasking habit. Go forth, Jedis.

Notes

1   S Furness, *Fly Higher: Train your mind to feel as strong as you look* (Rethink Press, 2022)

2   American Psychological Association, 'Multitasking: Switching costs' (APA, 20 March 2006), www.apa.org/topics/research/multitasking, accessed 21 May 2024

3   KP Madore and AD Wagner, *Multicosts of Multitasking* (Cerebrum, April 2019), www.ncbi.nlm.nih.gov/pmc/articles/PMC7075496/pdf/cer-04-19.pdf, accessed 12 May 2024

4   KF Lui, KH Yip and AC Wong, 'Gender differences in multitasking experience and performance', *Quarterly Journal of Experimental Psychology*, 74/2 (February 2021), https://doi.org/10.1177/1747021820960707

5   S Covey, *The 7 Habits of Highly Effective People: 30th anniversary edition (The Covey Habits)* (Simon & Schuster, 2020)

6   ASQ, 'Five whys and five hows' (ASQ Quality Press, no date), https://asq.org/quality-resources/five-whys, accessed 2 June 2024

7   J Moore, *Behind Enemy Lines* (Davis Entertainment, 2001)

8   D Avrin, *The Morning Huddle: Powerful customer experience conversations to wake you up, shake you up and win more business!* (Classified Press, 2021)

9   T Scott, *Top Gun* (Paramount Pictures, 1986)

10 J Kosinski, *Top Gun: Maverick* (Paramount Pictures, 2022)

11 L Becker, HC Kaltenegger, et al, 'Physiological stress in response to multitasking and work interruptions: Study protocol', *PLoS One*, 17/2 (8 February 2022), https://doi.org/10.1371/journal.pone.0263785

12 D Kahneman, *Thinking, Fast and Slow* (Penguin, 2012)

13 M Cay, C Ucar, et al, 'Effect of increase in cortisol level due to stress in healthy young individuals on dynamic and static balance scores', *Northern Clinics of Istanbul*, 5/4 (29 May 2018), https://doi.org/10.14744/nci.2017.42103

14 V Sawhney, 'Why we continue to rely on (and love) to-do lists', *Harvard Business Review* (3 January 2022), https://hbr.org/2022/01/why-we-continue-to-rely-on-and-love-to-do-lists, accessed 21 June 2024

15 A Pietrangelo, 'What the Yerkes-Dodson law says about stress and performance', *Healthline* (22 October 2020), www.healthline.com/health/yerkes-dodson-law, accessed 23 May 2024

16 BiteSize Learning, 'Navigating the "comfort, stretch, and panic zones" at work' (no date), www.bitesizelearning.co.uk/resources/comfort-zone-stretch-zone-panic-zone, accessed 23 May 2024

17 D Greenberger and CA Padesky, *Mind Over Mood: Change how you feel by chaining the way you think* (Guildford Press, 2016)

18 You can refer to them as IAs if you want to speak the lingo – we're not terribly imaginative in how we come up with nicknames in the RAF. We either abbreviate them to letters (eg, Doneth Hiller becomes DH) or we put an 'ee' sound on the end (so Bews becomes Bewsey). If we're feeling really exotic, we might put an 'oh' sound on the end (eg, Milne becomes Milno). It's pretty basic stuff, but bizarrely, rather sought after. There is no greater insult in the RAF than to be so unremarkable that you don't even warrant an extra vowel sound on your name.

19 The Policy Institute and the Centre for Attention Studies, *Do We Have Your Attention? How people focus and live in the modern information environment* (King's College London, 2022), www.kcl.ac.uk/policy-institute/assets/how-people-focus-and-live-in-the-modern-information-environment.pdf, accessed 24 May 2024

20 S Maybin, 'Busting the attention span myth', BBC News (10 March 2017), www.bbc.co.uk/news/health-38896790, accessed 24 May 2024

21 C Johnson, 'Stuck on negative thinking' (Care Counselling, no date), https://care-clinics.com/stuck-on-negative-thinking, accessed 24 May 2024

22 M Williams and D Penman, *Mindfulness: A practical guide to finding peace in a frantic world* (Piatkus, 2011)

23 R Doherty, SM Madigan, et al, 'The sleep and recovery practices of athletes', *Nutrients*, 13/4 (17 April 2021), https://doi.org/10.3390/nu13041330

24 D Pilat and S Krastev, 'The Eisenhower Matrix' (The Decision Lab, 2021), https://thedecisionlab.com/reference-guide/management/the-eisenhower-matrix, accessed 18 July 2024

25 G Keller and J Papasan, *The One Thing: The surprisingly simple truth behind extraordinary results* (John Murray, 2014)

26 T Ferriss, *The 4-Hour Work Week: Escape the 9-5, live anywhere and join the new rich* (Vermilion, 2011)

27 Cited during Productivity workshop for Yellow Door.

28 Anecdotal story used during the introduction of Flying Authorisers Course, Centre of Air Safety Training, MOD Shrivenham

29 I came up with this mostly from lived experience and an approximation of all the various texts I've read.

30 C Newport, *Deep Work: Rules for focused success in a distracted world* (Piatkus, 2016)

31 Friendly warning: use caution with anyone who uses the words 'mutual', 'synergies' or 'collaboration', or who is vague or verbose to the point of opaqueness about why they want a meeting. This is often code for, 'I don't yet have an established network of prospects and I'd like to steal yours.' These people will waste your time and attention and I'd hate for that to happen to you when you are working so hard to increase your productivity.

32 Forms part of the thirteen-course taster menu at Botrini's in Oia, Greece.

33 The 'two-minute-taskmaster' from the Pip Decks Productivity Tactics set: https://pipdecks.com

34 J Murphy, *The Power of Your Subconscious Mind* (Wilder Publications, 2011)

35 T Ferriss, *The 4-Hour Work Week: Escape the 9-5, live anywhere and join the new rich* (Vermilion, 2011)

36 From the Pip Decks Productivity Tactics set: https://pipdecks.com

37 www.focusmate.com

38 L Morgan, *More Balls Than Most: Juggle your way to success with proven company shortcuts* (Infinite Ideas, 2011)

39 JA Kent, 'Is it time to leave your comfort zone? How leaving can spark positive change' (Harvard Summer School, 24 May 2023), https://summer.harvard.edu/blog/leaving-your-comfort-zone, accessed 2 June 2024

40 W Stone, *Platoon* (Metro-Goldwyn-Mayer, 1986)

41 G Keller and J Papasan, *The One Thing: The surprisingly simple truth behind extraordinary results* (John Murray, 2014)

42 I use the word 'current' simply as a nod to that fact that my understanding of leadership is constantly evolving. (Another trait of good leadership is to be endlessly curious and keep learning.)

43 The 'campaign of influence' is my summary of all the best learning from military leadership, serving on the front line, being a parent, becoming a mindfulness coach and studying human factors.

44 S Covey, *The 7 Habits of Highly Effective People: 30th anniversary edition (The Covey Habits)* (Simon & Schuster, 2020)

45 Speech given to HCSA, 28 November 2023

46 My research is in its infancy at this stage and has been based on interviews and ChatGPT. So far, I've identified four strategies that are thought to help: being in healthy stress, having a hook, the work cycle and creating a focus fortress.

47 I Mills, *The Leader's Secret Code: The belief systems that distinguish winners* (LID Publishing, 2021)

48 G Keller and J Papasan, *The One Thing: The surprisingly simple truth behind extraordinary results* (John Murray, 2014); and C Newport, *Deep Work: Rules for focused success in a distracted world* (Piatkus, 2016)

Acknowledgements

My sincere thanks to AnnMarie Wyncoll, my book coach, who agreed to work with me on my second book. She helped me to stay on course and believe in myself when I thought I was wasting my time (and everyone else's, which is definitely not the point of the book).

Thanks to the team at Rethink, Sandra Smith, Kathleen Steeden and Anke Ueberberg, who helped me get this book into your hands. Their diligence, patience and gentleness with me has helped ease the process enormously.

Thank you to my friends and family, especially Emily, DH, Jamie and Aileen, who have supported me in the background and humoured me when I've climbed onto my soapbox.

Special mention to my two favourite boys: my partner Tim, who gets out of my way when I need uninterrupted uni-tasking time but is also available when I want to brainstorm, and my son Arthur, who calls me out when I'm not being present and/ or spending too much time on LinkedIn. (I remember when I was cool – those were the days.)

Finally thank you to my amazing clients and followers. The unexpected messages that pop into my inbox, or the person that stops me in the corridor to tell me how I've helped them – this is why I do it. While I believe in what I do, it's invaluable to me to hear that it's working for you too.

The Author

Sarah Furness is an ex-helicopter pilot in the RAF, a mindfulness coach and a motivational speaker. During her experiences, both at war and at home, she learned that tough, capable people don't always feel as strong as they look. She includes herself among them. This led her to develop the Healthy Automatic Behaviours In Threatening Scenarios (HABITS) formula – a blend of mindfulness and military combat techniques that can be used to train the mind to be bombproof under pressure and feel awesome at the same time.

She has a young son whom she adores and who inspires her every day.

🌐 www.sarahfurness.com

🌐 www.wellbeitcoach.com

in www.linkedin.com/in/sarah-furness-7173a538

◻ @wellbeitcoach